APL: A SHORT COURSE

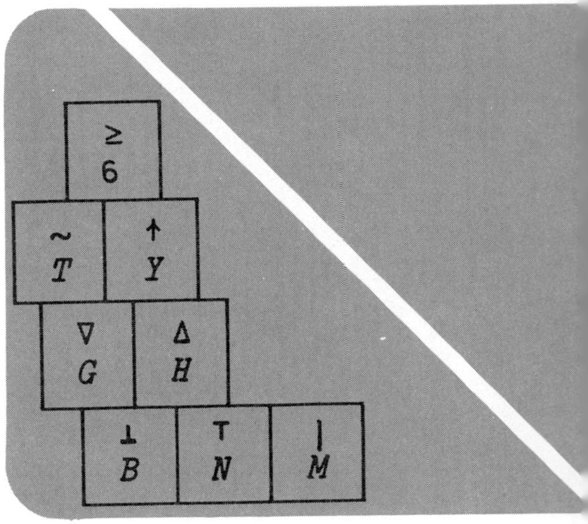
≥
6
~
T
↑
Y
∇
G
Δ
H
⊥
B
⊤
N
|
M

APL: A SHORT COURSE

SANDRA PAKIN

and the

STAFF OF COMPUTER INNOVATIONS

PRENTICE-HALL, INC., ENGLEWOOD CLIFFS, NEW JERSEY

Library of Congress Cataloging in Publication Data

PAKIN, SANDRA
APL: a short course.

Bibliography: p.
1. APL (Computer program language) I. Computer
Innovations. II. Title.
QA76.73.A27P35 001.6′424 73–5604
ISBN 0–13–038877–7

10 9 8 7 6 5 4 3 2 1

Printed in the United States of America

PRENTICE-HALL INTERNATIONAL, INC., *London*
PRENTICE-HALL OF AUSTRALIA, PTY. LTD., *Sydney*
PRENTICE-HALL OF CANADA, LTD., *Toronto*
PRENTICE-HALL OF INDIA PRIVATE LIMITED, *New Delhi*
PRENTICE-HALL OF JAPAN, INC., *Tokyo*

CONTENTS

LESSON 4 -- BRANCHING

LESSON 5 -- ITERATIVE FUNCTIONS, CONVERSATIONAL FUNCTIONS, AND CHARACTER HANDLING

LESSON 6 -- INTRODUCTION TO THE MATRIX

LESSON 7 -- USING MATRICES AND OTHER APL CAPABILITIES

PREFACE

APL: A Short Course was developed to meet the needs of Computer Innovations customers to learn APL, A Programming Language, and the use of APL defined functions quickly and easily. APL: A Short Course provides instruction in the salient features of APL:

1. Ordinary computation facilities
2. Function definition
3. Using defined functions
4. Handling arrays
5. Handling numeric and character data

The reader should be able to program most of his problems in APL after completing the lessons and doing the exercises. He should also be able to extend his APL knowledge by experimenting on his own, by referring to reference documents like the APL/360 Reference Manual, and by reading APL operational supplements like Computer Innovations' FMS (File Management System) Concepts which explains how the user can deal with large volumes of data under program control. Reading programs written in APL should also help the reader add to his APL expertise. A short bibliography of supplementary materials is included to guide the reader.

APL: A Short Course is organized in seven lessons with accompanying exercises. It is written predominantly in the second person to enhance the expectation that the reader is participating actively in the lessons. Thus, examples usually suggest that the reader try particular expressions at the terminal to see for himself what happens. In this way he can begin to experience the ease of computing in the interactive APL environment. Those expressions that should be tried at the terminal are indicated by a check mark (✓) at the left margin. Of course, the reader should feel free to experiment and try any other expressions he wishes.

The exercises are keyed to sections of each lesson. They should be done as indicated following the corresponding text section. Each lesson has a summary. Following the summary are solutions to the lesson's exercises.

Appendix A lists the functions and variables that the lessons refer to. These should be entered in the system (if not Computer Innovations') as they are shown before the exercises and examples of Lessons 2 through 7 are tried on the terminal. Moreover the reader should have a workspace available to him in which he can save his work from session to session. Appendix B provides three additional problems requiring longer solutions. And Appendix C is a list of the 47 APL primitive functions discussed in the lessons.

ACKNOWLEDGEMENTS

The rationale of the lessons in APL: A Short Course is the joint efforts of Sandra Pakin and Computer Innovations staff members Jean Franz, Joseph Mill, and Lawrence Mysz. Lessons 1, 2, 4-7 were written by Sandra Pakin. Jean Franz wrote Lesson 3 and provided valuable additions and critical comments to all the lessons.

We are grateful to the entire staff of Computer Innovations, and their enthusiastic APL customers, for their comments and cooperation.

APL:
A SHORT COURSE

LESSON 1 GETTING STARTED

Lesson 1 establishes a minimal set of techniques necessary to use APL on a terminal for evaluating ordinary arithmetic expressions.

Section 1.1 USING THE APL TERMINAL

The APL terminal is a typewriter-like device used in conjunction with an acoustic coupler to communicate over telephone lines with the APL computer system. There are a number of teleprocessing terminals with which APL can be used; for example, IBM 2741 and Datel 30. The keyboard description is based on the APL/360 keyboard which is produced by using the IBM 987 or 988 typeball. The procedures for using each terminal vary slightly and so the procedures given below for signing on and off are necessarily general; modification for the type of equipment you are using may be required and should be given to you.

The Keyboard. A diagram of the keyboard is shown in Figure 1 with the alphabet set you will use in your APL work. The key designations on the terminal should be either on the key tops or on the tabs on the fronts of the keys.

Figure 1. APL Keyboard

As you look at the keyboard diagram, you will notice that the <u>unshifted</u> letters and numbers (those on the lower portion of each key) are in the same position that they are on a regular typewriter. If you can touch-type, you should continue to do so, as much as possible. The symbols in the <u>shifted</u> position (those on the upper portion of each key) are mainly APL function symbols. The shifted symbols are produced by holding the shift key while striking the key containing the symbol.

<u>Signing On</u>. Before you can communicate with the computer, you must sign on. <u>Signing on</u> establishes a connection with the computer. <u>Signing off</u> terminates the connection. Following are the procedures for signing on and off.

Procedure for Signing On

The typewriter-terminal needs paper, the APL typeball, and a ribbon.

I. CHECK SWITCHES

1. PLUGS IN -- Make certain that the terminal and acoustic coupler are plugged into the wall socket and that the coupler is plugged into the terminal.

2. COUPLER OFF -- Turn the acoustic coupler to <u>off</u> by flipping the switch down. You should hear no sound from the coupler.

3. MARGIN SET -- Set the left margin indicator on the terminal to the margin desired; set the right margin indicator as far to the right as it will go.

4. PAPER IN -- Insert paper into the terminal.

5. TERMINAL ON -- Turn the terminal <u>on</u> by flipping the on-off switch on the keyboard. You should hear the hum of the terminal motor.

6. SWITCH ON REMOTE -- Check to see that the remote-local switch is on <u>remote</u>; if not, flip it to <u>remote</u>.

II. DIAL UP

7. DIAL -- Pick up phone and dial ___________*; you will hear a high-pitched tone. (Note: dial for an outside line first, if necessary.)

8. HEADSET IN COUPLER -- After you hear the high-pitched tone, insert the phone headset into the acoustic coupler, making sure that the cord end is on the correct side. Close the lid if the coupler has a lid.

9. COUPLER ON -- Turn the on-off switch on the coupler to <u>on</u>. If your terminal has lights, the blue and green lights should light.

III. SIGN ON

10. READY BY RETURNING -- Press the RETURN key on the terminal. Wait for the "proceed" light to light. (If your terminal has no lights, wait until the keyboard unlocks; you should not have to wait long.) Press the RETURN key on the terminal again. Wait for the green light or keyboard unlock.

11. SIGN-ON NUMBER -- Type your sign-on number. It is)___________* and press RETURN. Be sure to type) first. You must shift for this character. The computer responds with a sign-on message like the one shown.

*Insert appropriate numbers.

```
046)  8.36.43 02/05/72 COMIN

   A P L \ 3 6 0
```

When the sign-on message has printed and the keyboard releases (proceed light goes on), you are ready to proceed.

12. (optional) WIDTH SET -- The computer prints a line width of a maximum 120 spaces. To change the width from 120 spaces to some other width, perhaps to 70 spaces to accomodate 8-1/2 inch wide paper with a 10 space left margin and a 5 space right margin, type:

```
)WIDTH 70
```

70 can be replaced with any number between 30 and 120. The computer responds with the message:

```
WAS 120
```

indicating what the previous width setting was.

13. (optional) DIGITS SET -- The computer automatically prints ten significant digits, if an answer requires it. This can be changed from ten to any number between 1 and 16 with the command *)DIGITS N*, where *N* is a number between 1 and 16. For example, *)DIGITS* 5 changes significant digits to 5. This command like the *)WIDTH* command can be entered at any time. The response is the former digits setting.

Procedure for Signing Off

1. *)OFF* -- Type *)OFF* and press RETURN. The computer responds with a sign-off message like the following:

```
046   14.58.25  02/05/72  COM
CONNECTED       0.12.34   TO DATE    2.43.14
CPU TIME        0.00.07   TO DATE    0.04.27
```

2. SWITCHES OFF -- Turn off the terminal and acoustic coupler.

3. HANG UP PHONE -- Remove telephone from coupler and hang up.

Section 1.2 USING APL

Try signing on, signing off, and signing on again to familiarize yourself with the procedures.

Having signed on, you are now ready to use the computer. You can use the keyboard numbers and symbols to form expressions for evaluation. For example, to find the sum of 937 and 861, you would type the line

```
      937+861
```

and press RETURN. Whenever you want an expression that you have typed in acted on, you must press RETURN. After RETURN is pressed, the keyboard locks until the computer response is finished. The computer responds at the left margin, linefeeds, indents six spaces, and releases the keyboard for a new entry, like this:

```
      937+861       ←you type
1798                ←computer responds

      ↑             ←carrier waits here with keyboard released
```

In general, as you look at the terminal printout you can tell the difference between input--what you type--and output--what the computer responds with--because input is indented and output is not.

Each of the expressions below is made up of a number, called an argument, an operator, called a function, and another argument. They demonstrate how the functions of adding, subtracting, dividing, and multiplying are expressed in APL. For practice, try entering each expression to see what its value is. Be sure to press RETURN after completing each line.

```
√     17+42

√     31.5-9.68

√     100÷3

√     47.9×11.235
```

A Word About Errors. Until you become familiar with the keyboard, and even afterwards, it is not unlikely that you will be making some typing errors. Fortunately, correcting these errors is quite easy. The first procedure given below is used if you see the error before you have entered the expression; the other is used if an error report is sent by the computer.

Procedure for Error Correction
Before You Have Pressed RETURN

Backspace up to and including the error and press the interrupt key. Type in the correction and whatever should follow it. For practice, try this:

✓

```
93.2÷7.3
```

But do not press RETURN. Now change the divide to plus by backspacing, interrupt, and typing +7.3. The printout should look like this:

```
      93.2÷7.3
          ∧
          +7.3
100.5
```

Procedure for Error Correction
After You Have Pressed RETURN

The error report pinpoints the probable error type and location. It can be ignored. For example, suppose you had pressed RETURN before you had completed the expression 7.6×3.

```
      7.6×              ←RETURN pressed
SYNTAX ERROR            ←computer responds
      7.6×
        ∧
```

To correct the error, simply retype the line, correcting the errors.

```
      7.6×3
22.8
```

Some Uses. The following examples show how APL expressions can be used to solve some problems. In these examples, the problem is first stated in words. Then an expression that solves the problem is given. You should enter this expression at your terminal, and get a result from the computer.

Following the expression is a comment about the expression or the result, if necessary.

Example 1: Find the earnings per share of a company which made $1,296,547.21 and has 7,902,318 shares outstanding.

√

```
1296547.21÷7902318
```

No commas may be used in entering a single number. The decimal point is the period found on the bottom row of the keyboard, second key from the right. The divide sign ÷ must be used for division.

Example 2: Find the number of seconds in a year.

√

```
365×24×60×60
```

More than one use of a function can occur in the same expression.

Example 3: Find the amount of money you are in the red if you write a check for $38 when you have only $35.37 in your checking account.

√

```
35.37-38
```

A negative number is indicated by a raised bar ¯, for example, ¯2. The symbol ¯ is found on the shifted portion of the 2-key. A middle bar - is used to represent subtraction. The symbol - is found on the shifted portion of the +-key. For example, 12-18 is ¯6. Try the following expressions for practice with negative numbers:

```
√  67-98
√  ¯4-¯3
√  ¯5+20
√  5×¯5
```

Example 4: You are at the grocery store. Find the cost of 6 apples at 6 cents each, 2 cartons of milk at 60 cents each and 12 cans of tomato paste at 13 cents each.

✓

```
6  2  12 × .06 .6 .13
```

The list of numbers to the left of the times sign (×) is a list of the quantities of the three items being purchased. The list of numbers to the right of × is a list of the costs of the three items. The result is a list of prices, one total price for each item. A list of numbers like these is called a vector. Each number or element in a vector is separated from the others by at least one space. Here are a few more expressions with vectors for you to try:

```
✓   2  4  6 + 1  3  5
✓   6  3 ÷ 3  2
✓   9  4  7 × ¯2 ¯1  3
```

Section 1.3 WRITING AND EVALUATING EXPRESSIONS

As you have probably realized, an important aspect in learning to express what you want done on the computer is knowing how to formulate expressions that will cause the computer to make the intended evaluation. When only one operation is involved, as it was to find the checking account balance after one transaction in Example 3, there is little difficulty. But suppose you want to find the new balance after two withdrawals of $10 and $15 have been made from an account which had a balance of $39. Which expression when typed into the computer will give you the correct result of 14?

39-10-15 or 39-10+15

The answer, of course, depends on how the computer evaluates the expression. If you enter 39-10-15, you will see that the computer response is 44, clearly not the anticipated answer. On the other hand, the computer responds with the desired answer of 14 to the expression 39-10+15.

Expressions are written in such a way that they are read from left to right. So 39-10+15 can be read as "39 less the sum of 10 and 15" or as "subtract the sum of the two withdrawals from the balance". What this means for the evaluation of the expression is that the expression is evaluated from right to left; the rightmost function is performed first, then the next rightmost, and so on.

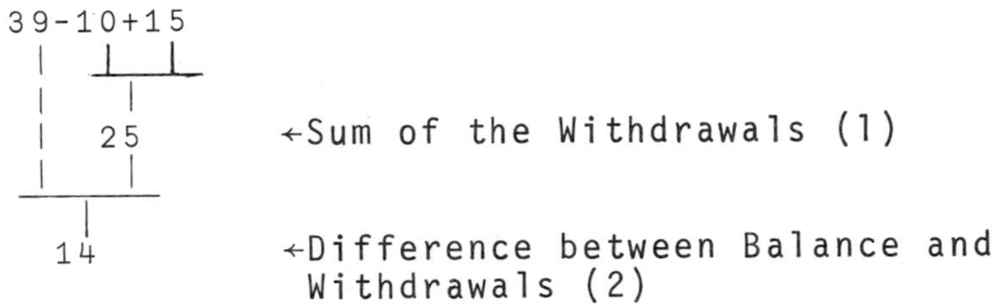

Let us look at another example. Suppose we want to find the discount if an item that generally costs $19.95 is reduced to $15.95. What we want then is 100 times one less the ratio of the reduced price to the original price. The solution expression can be written as:

```
100×1-15.95÷19.95
```

This will be evaluated from right to left as shown below.

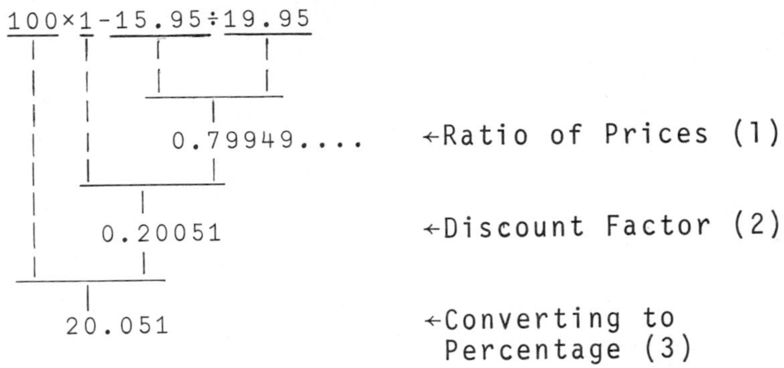

<u>Parentheses</u>. Parentheses can be used to change the order of execution of an expression. The functions in parentheses are performed first; then the execution proceeds from right to left. How using parentheses affects the evaluation of an expression is shown by means of the following example. Suppose you are purchasing a fleet of cars. You buy three Mercedes-Benz 280 SL's for $7478 each and five Maseratis for $18,550 each. How much does the fleet cost?

```
3×7478+5×18550          or          (3×7478)+5×18550
```

The value of the first expression is 300684 (for that kind of money you could buy 16 Maseratis). The parentheses are necessary, as shown in the second expression, to get the correct answer, a reasonable 115184. The evaluation of the second expression is shown step-by-step below.

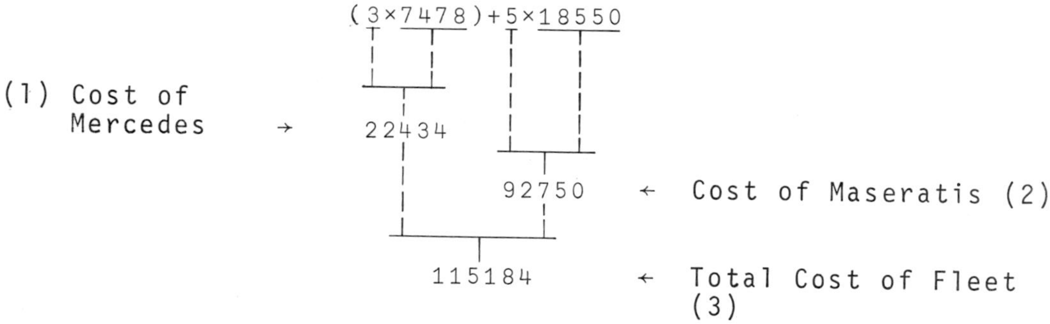

Using extra sets of parentheses does not affect the execution of an expression. So (3×7478)+(5×18550) also gives the correct result of 115184. When you are in doubt about how an expression will be evaluated, it is always best to use parentheses.

Parentheses can be used to "debug" (correct) the expression 39-10-15 from the checking account problem shown on page 8. Rephrasing the solution suggests a way of getting the correct result: "subtract the first withdrawal from the balance, then subtract the second withdrawal from that imtermediate balance". The solution with parentheses is:

✓
```
(39-10)-15
```

Try it.

Evaluating Expressions with Vectors. In general operations on vectors are performed by performing the function on the corresponding members of the vectors. For example:

```
      3 5 8+6 9 12
9  14  20
```

The vector result 9 14 20 is the result of adding 3 to 6, 5 to 9, and 8 to 12. The answer to a problem such as this one will have as many components as the vector argument(s) have numbers. Each vector argument must have the same number of elements as in Example 4 (otherwise the computer will give a *LENGTH ERROR* report) or one argument must be a single number, as in 12×6 8 5 whose result is 72 96 60.

Try these vector expressions yourself:

```
✓    3  5  8+6  9  12
✓    12×6  8  5
```

Then try the following expressions:

```
✓    4  6  8÷2                   ¯9-6 ¯2  1
✓    4  6  8÷2  3  4             7 5 3 5×0 5 2 7
✓    4  6  8÷2  3                1.6  ¯3 +1.2  4.1
```

The last example of the left column shows you what a *LENGTH ERROR* report looks like.

In an expression that contains several functions and one or more vector arguments, the vector argument is treated as one quantity and evaluation still proceeds from right to left. For example:

```
      8  3  7 × 6  2  1+5  9  2
88  33  21
```

The result is obtained as follows:

> The first number of the result vector is the result of evaluating the expression 8×6+5.
>
> The second number of the result vector is the result of evaluating the expression 3×2+9.
>
> The third number of the result vector is the result of evaluating the expression 7×1+2.

Until you become familiar with using vectors, you might find it helpful to use parentheses to delimit the vectors. For example, writing

```
      (8 3 7)×(6 2 1)+(5 9 2)
```

may help you see that the expression is of the form *A×B+C* and follows the right-to-left evaluation rule.

Some More Uses. Follow the instructions given with Examples 1 through 4, pages 7 and 8.

Example 5: Find the cost of a $435 color TV set for which an 18% discount has been given.

√

```
435-435×.18
```

The same result could be obtained by the expression:

√

```
435×1-.18
```

To find the cost including a 5% sales tax, enter:

√

```
1.05×435×1-.18
```

Example 6: Find the number of calories in eight ounces of fried shrimp if 3.5 ounces have 105 calories.

√

```
105×8÷3.5
```

Example 7: Find the ratio of each number in a list to the sum of numbers.

√

```
81 75 62÷81+75+62
```

Example 8: Find the scores for four students who got 113, 107, 139, and 85 points, respectively, out of a possible 150 points.

√

```
100×113 107 139 85÷150
```

Multiplying by 100 simply converts the ratio of student points to total points to a percentage.

Example 9: The delivery charge for groceries is 6-1/2% of the total bill excluding tax for those items being delivered. How much does a shopper pay altogether if $23.55 in groceries is delivered out of a total grocery charge before tax of $35.78. Assume a 5% sales tax.

```
(.065×23.55)+1.05×35.78
```

EXERCISES

Construct one-line expressions and evaluate them at the computer for the following problems. If the expression is correct, the result will agree with the given result. Otherwise read the summary on the following pages and try again. If you still have no success, compare your expression with that given in the solutions section at the end of this lesson.

1. The number of seconds in the month of March.

   Result: 2678400

2. The price per ounce of a carton of eight 16-ounce Pepsis selling for $1.11 a carton.

   Result: .008671875

3. Income tax due on taxable income of $6732.57. (Assume that the tax is $1130 plus 25% of the excess over $6000.)

   Result: 1313.1425

4. Balance after you have deposited $75 to make up for a $23 deficit in your checking account.

   Result: 52

5. The number of calories in 15 ounces of skim milk, regular milk, and chocolate milk if 8 ounces of skim milk has 88 calories, 8 ounces of regular milk has 166 calories, and 8 ounces of chocolate milk has 235 calories.

   Result: 165 311.25 440.625

6. The yearly interest on four savings accounts. The amounts in the accounts are $375, $973, $1023, and $1715. The interest rates are 5%, 4.25%, 4.5% and 4.75%, respectively.

   Result: 18.75 41.3525 46.035 81.4625

Section 1.4 SUMMARY

Numbers are represented in the usual way, except that no commas are used. For example, five thousand, six hundred, thirty-two is written 5632, not 5,632. The negative sign ¯ is used for representing numbers whose value is less than 0; for example, 6-7 is ¯1.

The arithmetic operations are represented by the symbols + - × ÷. Other symbols for these functions are not permitted, and multiplication signs cannot be omitted.

The same function can be performed on lists of numbers. We call these lists vectors. For example:

```
      3  5  8+6  9  12
9  14  20
```

The result vector is the result of adding each member of one vector to the corresponding member of the other vector.

It is also possible to have one argument a single number and one argument a vector. For example:

```
      .15×12  6  9
1.8  0.9  1.35
```

The result vector is the result of multiplying each member of the vector by .15.

Expressions are executed from right to left. Parentheses can be used to change the order of execution.

Section 1.5 SOLUTIONS

1. `31×24×60×60`

   The number of seconds is the product of the number of days in March (31), the number of hours in a day (24), the number of minutes in an hour (60), and the number of seconds in a minute (60).

2. `1.11÷8×16`

   The price per ounce is the quotient of the total price ($1.11) divided by the total ounces (8x16).

3. `1130+.25×6732.57-6000`

   Tax is 1130 plus 25% of the excess (6732.57-6000).

4. `75+¯23`

5. `88 166 235×15÷8`

   The list of calories in the base quantities (88 166 235) times the ratio of the given quantity to the base quantity (15÷8).

6. `375 973 1023 1715×.05 .0425 .045 .0475`

   The list of amounts times the list of rates converted from percents to decimals.

LESSON 2

DEFINED FUNCTIONS AND DATA

Lesson 1 had you doing most of the work--formulating expressions that would answer problems. At times, however, you will want to use a set of expressions called a program or defined function written and stored for you, where your only task at the terminal will be to provide the data that you want operated on. For example, you may wish to enter salary data into a payroll program that computes net pay. This lesson will give you experience in using previously defined functions and handling the data for them.

Section 2.1 USING DEFINED FUNCTIONS

In order to use a previously defined function you must know

1. Its name
2. How to bring it into your work area, called your active workspace
3. How to use it, that is, what form of data it expects

The name of a defined function is a name made up of alphabetic and numeric characters chosen by the programmer to serve as identification for a particular set of expressions. For example, the first defined function that you will use is called *GUESS*.

The way you will bring these functions into your workspace is called copying. Copying is done by a copy command. The copy command is formed by a right parenthesis), the word *COPY*, and information about what is to be copied and where it can be located. For example, type:

✓
```
)COPY __________* LESSONS GUESS
```

What this command does is to bring into your active workspace a copy of the defined function *GUESS* from a storage area called library ________* and stored workspace name *LESSONS*. If *GUESS* was copied into your active workspace, the computer responded with a *SAVED* message, telling you when the workspace *LESSONS* was last put into storage. (Sec. 2.3 discusses how to put work into storage.)

GUESS is a self-explanatory function. This means that you simply have to type *GUESS* and the program will tell you what you have to do and what will be done. Try it:

✓
```
GUESS
```

You may use the function *GUESS* as often as you like simply by calling it, that is, by typing its name.

GUESS is the kind of function that requires no information about how to use it. Other functions, such as the next one you will use, do require information. Bring the function *BESTBUY* into your active workspace by typing:

✓
```
)COPY __________* LESSONS BESTBUY
```

BESTBUY is a function that determines the most economical purchase of a list of items for which price and quantity in a fixed unit is provided. In order to use *BESTBUY* successfully you must provide the data as an argument. The data must be arranged in a vector where the first component is the price of the first item, and the second component is the quantity, the third is the price of the second item and the fourth is the quantity, and so forth for as many items as desired. For example, to determine the most economical purchase of three different packagings of a soft drink whose prices and sizes are

Insert the given library number here. Whenever ________ appears, it means to insert the given library number.

$1.11 for eight 16-ounce bottles
$ .15 for one 12-ounce can
$ .79 for six 10-ounce bottles

the expression

```
BESTBUY 1.11 128 .15 12 .79 60
```

Would be entered.†

The function *BESTBUY* determines the most economical purchase and prints a message telling the item number for the most economical. To see how this looks, type:

√

```
BESTBUY 1.11 128 .15 12 .79 60
```

Section 2.2 VARIABLES

If the function *BESTBUY* were used to determine which soft drink among the several available in the typical supermarket was the most economical, the data vector argument would be unwieldy. Several problems in entering the data as suggested might occur, for instance:

1. You may have more data to enter than can fit on a line.

2. You may make a typing error necessitating a cumbersome and time-consuming repair.

3. You may decide that you want to try a subgroup of data for comparison and would have to type many of the same numbers again.

4. You may want to use the data again to obtain some other information.

The best way to overcome any of these problems or potential problems is to store the data you want to work with as a variable. A variable is an alphameric name such as *T*, *DATA*,

†Typically, the workspace containing a function like *BESTBUY* would have a descriptive function or variable--called perhaps *BESTBUYHOW*--accompanying it. This would contain directions for using the function, such as those given in this paragraph.

or *S*128 which represents some data. A variable is defined by assigning to it some data. This is done by using the left-pointing arrow ← called specification. For example, type:

√
```
POP←1.11  128  .15  12  .79  60
```

This specifies the value of *POP* to be 1.11 128 .15 12 .79 60. If you type in the name of the variable, its value will be printed out. Type:

√
```
POP
```

If you make a mistake in typing the data for *POP*, reenter it. Now instead of keying in six numbers to provide data for *BESTBUY* you only have to key in *POP*. Try it:

√
```
BESTBUY POP
```

If you want to use *BESTBUY* with some new data, you can define a new variable, say *POP*1:

```
POP1←.45  32  .85  128
```

*POP*1 can also be used with *BESTBUY*. Try it:

√
```
BESTBUY POP1
```

Section 2.3 SAVING VARIABLES AND DEFINED FUNCTIONS

If you signed off after trying the examples of Sec. 2.1 or Sec. 2.2, and then signed on again, you found that the defined functions *GUESS* and *BESTBUY* and the variables *POP* and *POP*1 were no longer in your workspace. If you typed any of these names, you got a *VALUE ERROR* report. The reason is that signing off drops the active workspace and everything that was in it is lost.

The way to maintain your work from session to session is by saving your work in a storage workspace. Saving is done through the save command. Retrieval of the saved work is done through the load command or through the copy command.

These commands are known as <u>system commands</u>. System commands are that part of APL that is used to communicate with the APL system. They provide the means to store, retrieve, transfer, and erase work and to make inquiries about the contents of the active workspace.

The set of system commands given below will help you to

1. Establish a workspace in which to save your work on the lessons
2. Learn the basic system commands

The summary section restates the purpose of each command in convenient tabular form. Enter each command as it is shown. Sign on, if you haven't already, then:

```
√    )CLEAR
```

The command *)CLEAR* provides a clear, unused workspace--one which contains no variables or defined functions.

```
√    )WSID
```

The command *)WSID* returns the name of the active workspace. Since you typed *)CLEAR* just prior to typing *)WSID*, the active workspace name is *CLEAR WS*.

```
√    )SAVE APLXX
```

Replace *XX* with your initials, for example, *APLSP*

The name *APLXX* is the saved workspace's identification, its *WSID*. When the command is completed, the computer responds with a *SAVED* report, telling the time and date.

```
√    )WSID
```

The name associated with the active workspace now is the name of the saved workspace.

```
√    TEST←9 8 3

√    TEST
```

```
√      POP←1.11  128  .15  12  .79  60

√      POP

√      POP1←.45  32  .85  128

√      POP1

√      )VARS
```

The variables in the active workspace are listed alphabetically by the *)VARS* command.

```
√      )SAVE
```

The contents of the active workspace are saved in the storage workspace whose name is identical to that of the active workspace. This saving completely overrides what was stored previously.

```
√      )CLEAR

√      )SAVE
```

The diagnostic report indicates that it is not possible to use the command *)SAVE* if the active workspace is named *CLEAR WS*.

```
√      )SAVE APLXX
```

The diagnostic report indicates that before an update of a storage workspace can occur, the active workspace name must be the same as the storage workspace name.

```
√      )SAVE NEW
```

If you want to set up a new storage workspace, it does not matter what the name of the active workspace is.

```
√      )LIB
```

The library command *)LIB* lists the names of the workspaces in your storage area--your library.

You may have a workspace named *CONTINUE* in your library even though you never executed the command *)SAVE CONTINUE*. The workspace *CONTINUE* is automatically established if the terminal was disconnected before an *)OFF* command was given--perhaps because the terminal was shut off. The workspace *CONTINUE* contains the contents of the active workspace at the time the trouble occurred.

√ *)WSID*

The *)LIB* command is an inquiry command. It does not affect the name or the contents of the active workspace.

√ *)LOAD APLXX*

The *)LOAD* command retrieves the named workspace from the library and brings it into the active workspace. The load command overrides anything that was in the active workspace.

√ *)WSID*

The name of the active workspace becomes that of the loaded workspace.

√ *)COPY ____________ * LESSONS BESTBUY*

The *)COPY* command adds the object named to the active workspace.

√ *)FNS*

The functions in the workspace are listed alphabetically by the *)FNS* command.

√ *)VARS*

The *)COPY* command does not obliterate the active workspace. Whatever functions and variables are brought into the workspace by the copy command augment the functions and variables already in the active workspace. The *SAVED* report tells the time and date that the workspace copied from was last saved.

```
√   )WSID
```

The copy command does not change the name of the active workspace.

The copy command can be used to bring selective data from the library workspace into the active workspace, as it was above, or it can be used to bring all the data from the library workspace into the active workspace. If an object name is omitted from the copy command, all of the functions and variables in the named workspace are added to the active workspace.

Occasionally the object name in the copy command refers to a group of functions and variables. For example, in Lesson 3 when you execute

```
)COPY ____________* LESSONS BOWL
```

The functions *DIFFERENCE*, *MEAN*, *SUPER*, and *RANGE* and the variables *BOB*, *CAROL*, *TED*, and *ALICE* are copied into the active workspace. These names were grouped together by the *)GROUP* command. A description of this and all of the APL system commands can be found in the APL/360 Reference Manual.

```
√   )SAVE

√   )ERASE BESTBUY TEST
```

The *)ERASE* command removes the functions and/or variables named from the active workspace.

```
√   )FNS

√   )VARS

√   )COPY APLXX BESTBUY
```

The)*ERASE* command affected the active workspace but not the saved workspace. *BESTBUY* is still in the saved workspace *APLXX*.

```
√    )FNS
√    )VARS
√    )DROP NEW
```

The command)*DROP* removes a workspace from the library. A *DROPPED* report is printed, giving the time and date.

```
√    )LIB
√    )WSID
√    )FNS
√    )VARS
```

Dropping a workspace does not affect the active workspace.

You should now have a library workspace named *APLXX*. It should contain the function *BESTBUY* and the variables *POP* and *POP*1. From now on, each time you sign on to work on the lessons, you should load *APLXX*, and before signing off, you should save *APLXX*. The lessons make the assumption that you do this.

Using Other Peoples Libraries. Workspaces in other people's libraries can be loaded or copied provided you know the library identification number and the workspace name. In the load and copy commands the identification number precedes the workspace name. For example:

```
)LOAD 425142 HISSTUFF
```

It is not possible to save into another person's library or to drop a workspace in another person's library.

Section 2.4 MORE ABOUT VARIABLES AND VECTORS

If you entered the commands given in Sec. 2.3, you should have a workspace in your library named *APLXX*, where *XX* are your initials. *APLXX* should be the name of your active workspace. To verify this, type:

✓ `)WSID`

If the response is not *APLXX*, type:

✓ `)LOAD APLXX`

APLXX should contain the function *BESTBUY* and the variables *POP* and *POP*1. To make sure, try:

```
✓ )FNS
✓ )VARS
```

Suppose now that you want to combine the two sets of numbers; that is, you want to find the most economical item comparing the five items in *POP* and *POP*1. To do this, you can use the function <u>catenation</u>, which is represented by a comma. Type:

```
✓ POP,POP1
✓ BESTBUY POP,POP1
```

The result refers to the combined list.

POP and *POP*1 are still in the workspace in their original form, as you can see by typing:

```
✓ POP
✓ POP1
```

There are only two ways of changing the value of a variable:

1. Respecifying it. Anytime a variable name appears to the left of a specification, it is revalued. So:

```
✓ POP←.13 14 .46 32 .75 60
```

revalues *POP* as you can see if you type:

√ POP

2. Erasing the variable altogether. This is done with the erase command. Type:

√)ERASE POP

The erase command removed the name *POP* from the variable list and consequently its value. Type:

√ POP

You got a *VALUE ERROR* report because *POP* is no longer a name in the workspace. Type:

√)VARS

POP, as you can see, is not in the variables list. Replace *POP* by either typing:

√ POP←1.11 128 .15 12 .79 60

or:

√)COPY APLXX POP

If you want to retain the combined *POP* and *POP1* lists, you could set up another variable by typing:

√ CPOP←POP,POP1

√ CPOP

Or if you no longer cared about the individual lists, you might respecify one of the variables by typing:

√ POP←POP,POP1

√ POP

This will respecify *POP* to be the combined lists of *POP* and *POP*1. This is a good way of adding to a list without having to respecify numbers that you need. If you still have more data to add and you have reached the end of the line, you can add more data to the variable by typing, for example,

✓
```
POP←POP,.13 14 .46 32 .75 60
```

and in general:

NAME←*NAME*,additional data

Let us look at the variable *POP* once again.

```
      POP
1.11 128 .15 12 .79 60 .45 32 .85 128 .13 14 .46 32 .75 60
```

Each element in a vector can be identified by its position. For instance, 1.11 is element 1, or 1 is the <u>index number</u> of the element 1.11 in *POP*. Selecting an element out of a vector by naming its index number is known as <u>indexing</u> and is represented by an expression of the form:

NAME[index number]

The following expressions select specific elements out of *POP*. Enter each of them:

```
✓   POP[1]

✓   POP[5]

✓   POP[8]

✓   POP[1 5 8]

✓   POP[8 5 1]

✓   POP[1 1 1]
```

In the fourth expression, more than one component is selected. The result is a vector with as many components as there are numbers in the index expression. In the fifth expression, the components are selected in a different order. And in the last expression, the first component is selected three times. The result is a vector of three components, all the same.

One or more elements in a vector can be changed by respecifying that element. So if you want to change *POP*[1] to 1.23, you type:

```
√   POP[1]←1.23
```

Now look at *POP*:

```
√   POP
```

What does the expression

```
√   POP[2 6 9]←96 75 .17
```

do? Try it. Then type:

```
√   POP
```

Section 2.5 GENERATING SERIES OF NUMBERS

A primitive function that is useful for generating certain types of data is the index generator ⍳ (the symbol ⍳ is called iota). Index generator is a function of only one argument--a right argument. If you experiment with iota by trying various kinds of data as its argument, you will probably be able to figure out for yourself what it does. The expressions below test iota with positive integers, fractions, vectors, and negative integers. Try them to see how the computer responds.

```
√   ⍳10
√   ⍳8
√   ⍳15
√   ⍳2.1
√   ⍳1 2 3
√   ⍳¯7
```

As you saw, the index generator produces a vector of consecutive positive whole numbers (integers) from 1 through the argument. Index generator is a monadic function: it has one (mono) argument which appears to the right of the function symbol. (The functions studied in Lesson 1, + - × ÷ , are dyadic functions: each has two (dyad) arguments.) Index generator has a restricted domain; that is, the kind of argument it works on is limited: the argument must be a positive integer.

By using index generator, you can create various series of numbers. For example, try:

```
✓    2×⍳10
✓    ¯1+2×⍳10
✓    .1×⍳10
✓    11-⍳10
```

The first expression gives the first ten even numbers; the second, the first ten odd numbers; the third, consecutive tenths; and the last, a countdown from ten.

A general rule for creating a series like those above is

```
K+D×⍳E
```

where:

E is the number of elements you want in the series
D is the constant difference between consecutive elements in the series and
K is the difference between the first element of the series and *D*

Use the rule to write an expression for the series:
5 8 11 14 17 20 23 26

Try your expression on the computer, modifying it if necessary.

Index generator in conjunction with indexing can be used to select specific components from a vector. For instance, suppose you want to know the prices of the items in *POP*.

In other words, suppose you want every other element in *POP*. There are eight items represented in *POP*, so you want an expression for the first eight even numbers. This is

```
2×⍳8
```

2×⍳8 is an expression for the even index numbers of *POP*. The elements of *POP* in those positions can be seen by typing:

```
√    POP[2×⍳8]
```

These are indeed the prices. Name them *PRPOP*:

```
√    PRPOP←POP[2×⍳8]
√    PRPOP
```

Now write an expression for the quantities in *POP*; that is, the elements whose index numbers are odd, and store them in *QPOP*:

```
√    QPOP←POP[¯1+2×⍳8]
√    QPOP
```

What you have done now is select out certain elements of *POP*. With *PRPOP* and *QPOP*, you can perform a simple division to obtain the cost per unit for each of the eight items. Type:

```
√    PRPOP÷QPOP
```

EXERCISES

1. Evaluate the following by hand and check yourself at the computer.

```
5+⍳8

⍳8+5

⍳5÷2

¯.5+(⍳5)÷2×⍳5
```

2. Add a pair of parentheses to the second expression above to make it equivalent to the first.

3. Use index generator to generate the following vectors.

```
¯2  ¯1  0  1  2  3

22  32  42  52  62  72  82

.25  .5  .75  1  1.25  1.5  1.75  2  2.25  2.5
```

4. Enter the following and try to anticipate the results.

```
V←4  2  ¯3  1  0  6

V[4]

V[2 4]

V[4 2]

V[2 4 8]

V[1 2 3 4 5 6]

V[⍳6]

V[4 4 4 4]

V[V[1 3 6]]

V[3 4 6]←⍳3

V

V[4 3 6]←⍳3

V
```

5. Enter an expression to display the "reversal" of *V*, i.e., 6 0 1 ¯3 2 4

6. Evaluate the following:

```
3 4 6,9 6 2

T←4 7 15

R←6 2

M←¯1 3 ¯8 1
```

```
T,R

3 4,6+7

T,R,T,M

R,R

12÷T,R

T,12÷R

3 4 5 M

3 4 6,M

M 3 4 6

M,3 4 6

(12÷T),R

(6+7),3 4

(6+7) 3 4
```

7. Here are the prices and sizes in ounces for 20 general-purpose caulking compounds rated by a consumers' group:

Compound	Price	Quantity
A	.73	5.5
B	1.73	3.0
C	1.92	3.0
D	.96	3.5
E	.94	5.0
F	.99	6.0
G	1.11	11.5
H	.83	4.5
I	1.23	11.5
J	1.52	11.0
K	1.23	6.0
L	.39	11.0
M	.55	12.0
N	.38	11.0
O	1.42	11.5
P	.89	4.5
Q	1.19	6.0
R	.74	4.0
S	.81	11.0
T	.75	4.0

a. Store the price and quantity in a vector named *GPCC*. If all the numbers do not fit on the line, follow the instructions in the text for getting more than one line of data stored in a variable.

b. Display *GPCC* and proofread it. To help you, you may rearrange *GPCC* in a table by using the function *TABLE*:

```
)COPY __________* LESSONS TABLE
```

The form for *TABLE* is (*R*,*C*) *TABLE X* where *R* is the number of rows and *C* is the number of columns and *X* is the data. To display *GPCC* as a 20 row, 2 column table, type:

```
20 2 TABLE GPCC
```

Correct any errors by using indexing and specification.

c. Use the function *BESTBUY* to determine which compound is the most economical.

d. Compounds A-E are rated very good; F-I are rated good; J-Q are rated fair-to-good; and R-T are rated fair. Use the function *BESTBUY* to determine the most economical compound in each group.

Hint: Use the variable *GPCC* and indexing to select subgroups of data.

e. Produce a price per ounce vector of all the compounds.

Section 2.6 SUMMARY

System Commands.

Ten system commands were introduced in Lesson 2. They are as follows:

COMMAND	PURPOSE
)*VARS*	Lists names of variables in active workspace
)*FNS*	Lists names of functions in active workspace
)*LIB*	Lists names of workspaces in your library storage

)*WSID*	Gives name associated with the active workspace
)*ERASE* names	Erases variables and/or functions named
)*SAVE* name	Puts in library storage a workspace named name. Contents of name are the contents of the active workspace.
)*SAVE*	Saves the active workspace in the library storage workspace having the same name as the active workspace
)*LOAD* name	Brings into the active workspace a copy of the storage workspace name overriding whatever was in the active workspace.
)*COPY* name	Brings into the active workspace the variables and functions in the workspace name without overriding what is in the active workspace
)*COPY* name obj	Brings into the active workspace the variable or function named obj from the storage workspace name
)*DROP* name	Drops the storage workspace name from the library
)*CLEAR*	Makes the active workspace clear of all variables and functions

Note that the load command and the copy command can be used with other peoples libraries by including the library identification number after the command word. For example:

```
)COPY 456789 APLSP GUESS

)LOAD 456789 APLSP
```

Variables. Variables are specified by:

NAME←value

For example:

```
      TRS←16  32  14

      PMI←5.67890

      M←TRS-2
```

Typing the name of the variable causes its value to be printed printed. For example:

```
      TRS
16  32  14

      PMI
5.6789
```

Variables can be respecified by putting the variable name to the left of the arrow. For example:

```
      TRS←931
```

A variable can appear to the left and to the right of a specification. For example:

```
      TRS←TRS,31  9  82
```

The value of *TRS* is the value after catenating the old value of *TRS* and the vector 31 9 82. The value of *TRS* now is 931 31 9 82.

New Primitive Functions. The definitions of the primitive functions introduced in Lesson 2 are given below.

- Catenation *A*,*B*

A vector of the elements of *A* followed by the elements of *B*. For example:

```
      3,4
3   4

      2 1,7 89 5
2  1  7  89  5

      M←9 7 6 3
      N←2 1 7
      M,N,N
9  7  6  3  2  1  7  2  1  7
```

• Indexing *A*[*B*]

The elements of *A* whose index numbers are *B*. For example:

```
      TM←24  60  120  15  8
      TM[1]
24

      TM[3  4]
120  15
```

• Index Generator ⍳*B*

The integers from 1 through *B*. For example:

```
      ⍳8
1  2  3  4  5  6  7  8
```

Section 2.7 SOLUTIONS

Your answers to Exercises 1, 4, and 6 can be checked at the terminal.

2. `(⍳8)+5`

3. `¯3+⍳6`

   `12+10×⍳7`

   `.25×⍳10`

5. `V[7-⍳6]`

7. a. `GPCC←.73  5  .94  5  .96  3.5` etc.

   GPCC←*GPCC*, numbers left over

   b. *GPCC*[index of wrong number]←right number

   c. `BESTBUY GPCC`

   d. `BESTBUY GPCC[⍳10]`

   `BESTBUY GPCC[10+⍳8]`

   `BESTBUY GPCC[18+⍳16]`

   `BESTBUY GPCC[34+⍳16]`

   e. `GPCC[¯1+2×⍳20]÷GPCC[2×⍳20]`

LESSON 3 USING AND DEFINING FUNCTIONS

This lesson continues the discussion of using defined functions and develops the principles behind defining functions through the use of an extended example.

Section 3.1 USING A DEFINED FUNCTION CONTINUED

Suppose you are a member of a bowling team. At the first session you bowl 125, 142, 109, and 153. Before the averages are posted, you want to know your average (or mean) score. This, as you know, can be found by adding up the four scores and then dividing the sum by four.

✓ Execute a command that will compute your average for you.

Did you get the correct result of 132.25? If not, recall that the computer executes the command from right to left; you must use parentheses to alter this order of execution when necessary.

The next week you bowl 118, 171, 134, and 99.

✓ Use the computer to find your average for this session and your overall average for the two weeks.

After the second week, the record-keeper for the league leaves to join the marines and you are elected record-keeper. How long did it take you to compute your own average above?

Think how long it will take you to compute the averages of each of the sixty members of the league now--and after the tenth week, when each member has bowled about forty games. Mind-staggering, isn't it. But the former record-keeper tells you not to despair. He has defined an APL function to computer the averages that will save you a lot of work. It is named *MEAN* and is stored in __________ * *LESSONS*. Then he takes off. Soon after the next session, members of the league begin calling you to ask when the list of averages will be posted. You decide that you had better learn how to use *MEAN*. Here is how you might go about it.

Bring the function *MEAN* into your workspace by typing

√)*COPY* __________ * *LESSONS MEAN*

Your first task is, of course, to find out how to use *MEAN* to compute the averages. If no directions are provided, this can be done by experimenting with *MEAN*. The first step in determining how *MEAN* works is to determine the number of arguments on which it operates. If you use the wrong number of arguments, a *SYNTAX ERROR* report is displayed by the computer. You must be careful to leave a blank space between the function name and each of the arguments or you will receive an error report even though the number of arguments is correct.

Defined functions may have no arguments, one argument, or two arguments. To test for syntax, try:

√ *MEAN*

√ *MEAN* 2

√ 2 *MEAN* 2

The first and third of these commands should have produced an error report. Unfortunately, the second form--the one that gave no error report--does not give very illuminating information. Perhaps this is because we chose an inappropriate argument, even though we have the correct syntax. Since *MEAN* is going to be used to average a list of scores, we should probably try a vector argument instead of the scalar (single number) argument 2. For example:

√ *MEAN* 2 3 7

4 is indeed the average of 2, 3, and 7. Try another vector argument, one with a different number of components, for instance:

√ *MEAN* 4 7 2 5 3

√ *MEAN* 89 95 67 101

Then try using *MEAN* to compute the average score in your first bowling session.

√ *MEAN* 125 142 109 153

The computer should display the same answer that was displayed when you computed your average earlier without using *MEAN*.

A defined function, like *MEAN*, is defined with one, two, or no arguments. It must be used in the way it was defined. *MEAN*, as you discovered earlier, must be used with one argument. Most primitive APL function symbols, on the other hand, may be used with one argument--in which case, the symbol represents a monadic function--or with two arguments--in which case, the symbol represents a dyadic function. For example, the symbol ÷ can represent either a monadic function or a dyadic function:

	Monadic	Dyadic
Expression	÷2	3÷5
Result	0.5	0.6
Meaning	reciprocal (1÷2)	division

Let us continue. To save some typing store your first session's scores in the variable *ME*1.

√ *ME*←125 142 109 153

Now you can find your average by typing:

√ *MEAN ME*1

You can find your average for the second session by typing:

```
✓   ME2←118 171 134 99
✓   MEAN ME2
```

And you can find your cumulative average by typing:

```
✓   MEAN ME1,ME2
```

Recall that the comma catenates elements; that is, strings them together. You can, if you wish, store the cumulative scores by specification.

```
✓   CME←ME1,ME2
```

Then you can compute the average of *CME*:

```
✓   MEAN CME
```

✓ If your scores on the third week of bowling are 112, 145, 164, and 137, what is your average for this session? What is your overall average for the three sessions? Try it.

By now you can see how handy *MEAN* is going to be in your work with the bowling league, even though it took a little trouble to find out how to use it. Actually there is a way of finding out what the syntax of a defined function, such as *MEAN*, is without experimenting. Type:

```
✓   ∇MEAN[0⎕]∇
```

Looking at the whole line that types out:

```
[0]  Z←MEAN X
```

The [0] indicates that the following formation is the function header. The header itself--*Z←MEAN X*--gives the function syntax. *MEAN* is the name of the function; *X* stands for the argument of the function; and *Z←* means that the result is explicit.

A defined function with an explicit result can be used in an APL statement together with other functions. Suppose that after the first week's bowling your handicap is 51. (A bowling handicap is a number that is determined according to the rules of the bowling league. It is added to the poor bowler's score to enable him to compete with good bowlers. The handicap of a poor bowler is larger than that of a good bowler.) Totals are compared to determine the high scorer after the handicap has been added to the raw score. You wish to find your average for the second session and add it to your handicap. Recall that your second session scores are stored in variable *ME*2 and that the order of execution of a command is from right to left. Type:

√
```
51+MEAN ME2
```

You were able to add 51 to the result of *MEAN* operating on *ME*2 only because *MEAN* gives an explicit result. Let us see what happens with a function that does not give an explicit result. You should still have the function *BESTBUY* in your workspace. Type:

√
```
)FNS
```

to find out. If not, type:

√
```
)COPY ________* LESSONS BESTBUY
```

Once you have a copy of *BESTBUY*, type:

√
```
∇BESTBUY[0⎕]∇
```

Note that the header--*BESTBUY X*-- shows no explicit result, since no ← appears in it. Try executing:

√
```
BESTBUY 65 12 121 20
```

√
```
51+BESTBUY 65 12 121 20
```

There is only one way in which *BESTBUY* can be used--to print out an optimal purchase. *MEAN* with its explicit result can be used in three ways:

1. To display the result *MEAN ME*1

2. To store the result in a variable *D*←*MEAN ME*1

3. In combination with other functions in an APL statement 51+*MEAN ME*1

Section 3.2 LOOKING AT A DEFINED FUNCTION

Now that you know how to use *MEAN*, you might be curious as to how it works the way it does. This requires getting a display of the function. You already know that to see what's stored in a variable you merely type the name of the variable and its contents are displayed. To display a defined function requires a bit more typing. To display *MEAN*, type:

√ ∇*MEAN*[⎕]∇

The first line of a defined function which the computer displays is the function header. For purposes of identification in the definition of the function, names are given to the argument(s) and the result. These names are simply for reference while the function is being executed. You have already seen that *MEAN* can be used with variables *ME*1 and *ME*2 (and not necessarily *X*) and its results can be specified as variable *D* (and not necessarily *Z*). The *X* and *Z* of the *MEAN* function are, then, merely placeholders. However the name *MEAN* is not a placeholder.

The definition of *MEAN* appears in the line following the header:

```
[1]  Z←(+/X)÷⍴X
```

The definition, as you can see, contains two new primitive APL functions:

+/ and ⍴

To understand the *MEAN* function, you must determine what these two primitive functions do. This can be done by some selective experimentation.

You can see from the structure of the statement that both ⍴ and +/ use only one argument. You know from your experience in executing *MEAN* that the argument is a vector. You also know what must be done to find the mean of a set of numbers and that this combination of functions does it. With these clues and some experimentation, you should be able to determine how monadic ρ and +/ work. You can experiment by trying monadic ρ with various scalar and vector arguments. Use vectors with different numbers of elements and with elements of different values until you can predict the results for any argument. For example, try these:

√	ρ6 9 3 2	ρ¯62.3 24.5 6
√	ρ*ME*1	ρ*ME*2
√	ρ*ME*1,*ME*2	ρ6
√	ρ¯6	ρ5.1
√	ρ¯5.1	ρι10
√	ρ*ME*2[3]	ρ*CME*[2 4 6]

After you know what ρ does, try to determine what +/ does to various scalar and vector arguments. You might wish to try the / alone with scalar and vector arguments to see what happens. If you are not sure about the definitions of ρ and +/, refer to the summary where they are defined.

When you understand what the two new primitive functions do, you can try the following sequence of executions to see how *MEAN* operates on vector *ME*1:

```
√   ρME1
√   +/ME1
√   (+/ME1)
√   (+/ME1)÷ρME1
```

You might also be curious as to what would happen if the parentheses were removed. The order of execution would be affected, but would the results differ? Try:

```
√   ρME1
√   ME1÷ρME1
√   +/ME1÷ρME1
```

Can you see why the first sequence of executions is preferable to the second? If you execute the two sequences by hand, you will see why.

For your bowling league work, you might consider keeping all the scores for each bowler in one variable, since you are mainly interested in the cumulative average. You can get all of your scores for the first two weeks stored in variable *ME*1 by specifying:

```
√    ME1←ME1,ME2

√    ME1

√    ρME1
```

Because of the right-to-left sequence of execution of an expression, the computer knows that it is the previously specified value of *ME*1 which is to be catenated with the elements of *ME*2 to be stored as a new set of elements called *ME*1. If you want the first week's scores, you can now indicate:

```
√    ME1[1 2 3 4]
```

or:

```
√    ME1[⍳4]
```

to get the first four components of *ME*1 and:

```
√    ME1[5 6 7 8]
```

or:

```
√    ME1[4+⍳4]
```

to get the second set of four components.

Of course, it is not necessary to store this week's scores in a variable before catenating them onto the cumulative variable. To add the third week's scores you could type:

✓
```
ME1←ME1,112 145 164 137
```

How many elements are there in *ME*1 now? Use ⍴ to find out.

Section 3.3 DEFINING A FUNCTION

In addition to computing the averages of the members of the league, it is up to you to compute their handicaps. In this league, the handicap is 75% of the difference between the bowler's cumulative average and 200; no bowler in the league has an average greater than 200. The previous record-keeper has no function to help you here, but you can define one for yourself and store it in your workspace.

There are two things which you must decide before defining a function:

1. What you want to name your function
2. What syntax you wish it to have

The function name can be any combination of letters and numbers as long as the first character of the name is a letter. Suppose you decide to call the handicap function *HCAP*. You want it to have an explicit result *Q* (which will be the value of the handicap) and decide that since you will store scores as vectors, it will be most convenient if *HCAP* operates on the raw scores. Thus, *HCAP* will require one argument *A*--a vector of all previous bowling scores.

Now you are ready to enter function definition mode. Once in this mode, the computer will store the commands you enter now for execution later. The symbol ∇ (read "del") is used to change from execution mode to function definition mode, or vice versa. Enter ∇ and the header on one line:

✓
```
∇Q←HCAP A
```

The computer responds by displaying a bracketed one:

```
[1]
```

And waits for you to enter the statement (or statements) which will define the *HCAP* function. Clearly, to find the handicap, you need the mean of *A*. Since *MEAN* is a function with an explicit result, it can be used within the *HCAP* function to produce the mean. Complete the line which the computer began:

```
✓   [1]  Q←.75×200-MEAN A
```

When the computer responds with a bracketed two (indicating that it is ready to accept the second statement in the definition), enter a ∇ to return to execution mode (since the definition of *HCAP* requires no second statement):

```
✓   [2]  ∇
```

Now enter:

```
✓   )FNS
```

and note that the name *HCAP* has been added to the list, inserted in alphabetic order. Try *HCAP* with your scores, stored in *ME*1, to find your handicap after three weeks of bowling.

```
✓   HCAP ME1
```

If *HCAP* works, save *APLXX* to update its contents.

Like variables, any defined function can be eliminated at will. Delete *MEAN* (it can always be copied again from ________* *LESSONS*) by typing:

```
✓   )ERASE MEAN
```

Investigate the results of this deletion by entering:

```
✓   )FNS

✓   MEAN ME1

✓   HCAP ME1
```

Typing this last command results in a suspension of activity by the computer and the display of an error report. This is no longer due to an error in syntax, however, but occurs because the execution of *HCAP* requires the mean of the vector as computed by *MEAN*. Since *MEAN* no longer exists in your workspace, the value of the mean cannot be computed; execution of *HCAP* cannot proceed further without this value.

When function execution is suspended because of an error within the function definition, you can get out of trouble (you get back to where you were before entering the function) by entering:

✓ (→)

Try it. Then type:

✓ |)*COPY* ________* *LESSONS MEAN* |

to bring *MEAN* back into your workspace.

You have seen that function definition is much like writing on the blackboard--you can define a function and then erase it at will. While you are defining the function, you can correct any error you make in the usual way, before hitting the return key. But what happens if you wish to alter something in your function after it has been entered? Such changes are easy to make.

To change something in the defined function that is not a part of the header, you can return to function definition mode by entering ∇ followed only by the name of the function. For example, suppose the handicap rule for the league changes, and handicaps are now based on 75% of the difference between the mean score and 250. *HCAP* should be altered to reflect this. Enter:

✓ (∇*HCAP*)

to return to function definition mode for this function. The computer responds with a bracketed two, ready for a second statement, if you choose to add one:

```
[2]
```

You wish only to change statement [1], however, so you enter the number of the statement you wish to replace, followed by the new version of the statement that you want. The display of the [2] supplied by the computer and your input together will look like:

✓ `[2] [1] Q←.75×250-MEAN A∇`

You may display the altered function by entering:

✓ `∇HCAP[⎕]∇`

If everything is not as you would like it, you can always repeat the above process and make changes, or even erase the entire function using the *)ERASE* command and start again.

Suppose the handicap rule changes again, now using 70% of the difference between the mean score and 250. It may be easier for you to enter the new line you want if you can see what the old line is. You can display the function and enter function definition mode all at once by entering:

✓ `∇HCAP[⎕]`

omitting the final ∇. The computer responds with a display of the function, as well as [2], waiting for your next entry. Notice that although the computer shows a ∇ as part of the display of the function, the displayed ∇ does not change the mode from function definition to execution. Only a ∇ typed and entered by you can do that.

✓ Change the function by inserting a new statement [1] to reflect the new handicap rule of the league, using the same technique as before. Remember to leave function definition mode by entering a ∇. Then try *)FNS*, display *HCAP*, and test *HCAP* on a vector of your choice.

If statement [1] of function *HCAP* were longer and more complex, you might not enjoy typing the entire statement to make a change. Suppose you prefer to name the function to compute means or averages *AVG*, rather than *MEAN*. You will have to change *HCAP* so that it uses *AVG* instead of *MEAN* to compute the average. To do this without retyping the entire line, enter:

✓ `∇HCAP[1⎕12]`

Note that with the initial ∇ you have again entered function definition mode. The computer responded with a display of the line of interest, and the typeball moved over twelve spaces. You can reposition the typeball by spacing and backspacing. Every character that you place a slash / under will be deleted. If you place a digit beneath a character, that many spaces will be inserted to the left of the character. Try:

```
  [1]   Q←.75×MEAN A          -- Computer typed this line
✓               ////3         -- You type this line
```

When you have returned, the line will be displayed again with the changes you indicated. At this time, you may make insertions. If you hit the index key, you will erase from that character on.

```
  [1]   Q←.75×     A          -- Computer typed this line

✓ [1]   Q←.75×AVG A           -- Same line, after you
                                 insert the new name
```

Close function definition by typing a ∇ when [2] appears. Display the new function *HCAP* and test it. What happened? You have not yet a function named *AVG* in your workspace. You can define one or you can edit the header of *MEAN* to change its name. To edit the header you use [0] as the statement number and then use either of the editing procedures described above. Don't forget to type → to get out of suspended execution before you execute *HCAP* again.

EXERCISES

1. a. Clear your workspace by entering:

```
✓      )CLEAR
```

then:

```
✓      )COPY ___________* LESSONS BOWL
```

BOWL is a group of functions and variables. Execute *)FNS* and *)VARS* to see what functions and variables you have copied. Each variable is a vector of bowling scores for a league member after five weeks of bowling. For simplicity, scores are stored for only a limited number of the members.

b. Find the number of games each member of Team #1 with scores stored in *BOB*, *CAROL*, *TED*, and *ALICE* has bowled.

c. Without using the addition function +, find the total number of games bowled by all the members of Team #1.

d. Find the average of each of the members of Team #1.

e. Find the handicap of each of the members of Team #1.

f. Find the total score for each member of Team #1 and for all the members as a group.

g. Find the team average for Team #1.

2. Instead of basing the handicap on 200 or 250, the league members have decided to base it on the highest average of any player. Since this number may change from week to week, it should be an argument of the handicap function *HCAP*. Redefine *HCAP* to have two arguments and an explicit result.

Hint: Header form might be ∇*Q*←*B HCAP A* where *A* is a vector of scores and *B* is the highest player average.

3. A number of primitive functions work in a manner similar to the arithmetic functions. By experimenting with various arguments determine what the following functions do.

a. *A*⋆*B*

b. *A*⌈*B*

c. *A*⌊*B*

d. !*B* (! is formed by ' backspace ..)

e. -*B*

f. ÷*B*

4. The function *DIFFERENCE* operates on any of the variables in your workspace. What does it do and how does it work? Feel free to display the function.

5. You have seen how +/, which we call <u>plus-reduction</u>, works. There are other kinds of reduction. Execute the following and use the results to assist you in seeing how other forms of reduction work.

```
√     +/2 ¯6 10          2+¯6+10
√     ×/2 ¯6 10          2×¯6×10
√     -/2 ¯6 10          2+6+¯10
√     2+10-¯6            ÷/2 ¯6 10
√     2÷¯6÷10            2×10÷¯6
√     */2 ¯6 10          */2 1 3
√     ,/2 ¯6 10
```

Feel free to experiment with other arguments. As you can see, there are several dyadic functions that may be used with reduction; that is, to the left of the /. Do you see why you cannot use the catenation function with reduction?

6. Execute the following, using a form of reduction:

a. Divide 24 by the sum of 7, 3, and negative 5.

b. Add 16 to the product of 5, 2, negative 11, and 3. (Recall that the result of a reduction operation is a value, and must be separated from other values by a function.)

7. *SUPER* is a handicap function that is based on 200, but will work for super bowlers with averages over 200, as well as for less skillful bowlers. Find what it does and how it works. You may have to experiment to find out what the new dyadic primitive APL function ⌈ does. Try ⌈ first with scalar arguments, since that is the kind it uses in *SUPER*.

a. What do you think will be the result of executing

```
4⌈5⌈2
```

Try it and see. Then try

```
⌈/4 5 2
```

Try some other cases until you see how ⌈-reduction works.

8. a. *RANGE* is an APL defined function to give the highest and lowest score of any bowler. How does it work? Can you shorten it? Leaving the header intact, modify *RANGE* to make the defining statement as short as possible.

b. Define a function that will display a vector whose

elements are (1) a bowler's average, (2) his handicap, (3) the number of games he has bowled, (4) his high score, and (5) his low score. You may incorporate any defined or primitive functions in your function.

c. Find the highest game bowled by *BOB*. By any member of Team #1. Find the lowest score bowled by *CAROL*. How much lower was it than her last score?

9. a. Write a function to give the absolute value of any number. Will it work for vectors of numbers? Test your function with different arguments.

b. Write a function to give the absolute value of the largest number in a vector. Test your function.

10. a. *WHICH* is a function that determines which of two bowlers has the higher average. It displays a ¯1 if the scores on the left have the lower mean and 1 otherwise. How does it work?

b. What happens in the case of a tie? Do you see a rather unconventional definition that has been incorporated in the language? Can you divide all numbers by zero in APL?

Section 3.4 SUMMARY

Determining How a Function Works. Without looking in a reference document, you can determine how many functions work by trying the function with different types of arguments and studying the results. Also displaying the definition of a defined function and trying different types of arguments with it makes it possible to determine how defined functions work. For either primitive or defined functions, you should try scalar and vector arguments, whole numbers--positive, negative, and zero--and fractional numbers. If you can predict what a result will be when a function is applied to certain arguments, you probably know what that function does.

Function Definition. Function definition mode is entered by typing a ∇ followed by the function header. The function header describes the syntax of the function. It must have a name; it may also have no, one, or two arguments, and it may have an explicit result. There are six forms of function header. These are shown below:

	With Explicit Result	Without Explicit Result
no arguments	∇Z←*NAME*	∇*NAME*
one argument	∇Z←*NAME ARG*	∇*NAME ARG*
two arguments	∇Z←*ARG*1 *NAME ARG*2	∇*ARG*1 *NAME ARG*2

The function's definition is entered statement by statement following the bracketed numbers displayed by the computer. Function definition is ended and execution returns to calculation mode by typing a ∇ at the end of a statement or following the bracketed number.

Function Editing. Various forms of function editing are shown in the table below.

TO--	BY ENTERING DEFINITION MODE--	WHILE IN DEFINITION MODE--
Display function	∇*NAME*[⎕]∇	[3][⎕]∇
Display a line	∇*NAME*[2⎕]∇	[3][2⎕]∇
Replace a line of the function	∇*NAME*[1] .....∇	[3] [1].......∇
Add a line to the end of the function	∇*NAME*	
	The computer responds with the number of the next statement to be added.	
Insert a line within the function	∇*NAME*[1.1].....	[3][1.1] ......
	This inserts the new line between statements 1 and 2. After definition is closed, statements are renumbered to consecutive integers.	
Erase a line	∇*NAME*[1] Interrupt/RETURN	[3][1] Interrupt/RETURN
	Nothing else can be typed on the line.	

TO--	BY ENTERING DEFINITION MODE--	WHILE IN DEFINITION MODE--
Character edit	∇*NAME*[3⎕6]	[4][3⎕6]
	The first number within brackets is the statement number; the second is the number of spaces from the left margin that the typeball should be positioned. Then: (1) Type / to delete character. Type digit to have that many spaces inserted to the left of the character. RETURN to have typeball positioned at end of line. (2) Enter new characters if any.	

New Primitive Functions. The primitive functions introduced in Lesson 3 are defined below.

• Shape *ρB*

This function counts the number of elements in a vector. If the argument is a scalar--a single number--rather than a vector, a blank line is shown.

• Plus-Reduction *+/B*

This function places a plus between each element in a vector and performs the resulting addition. If the argument is a scalar, the result is that scalar. Besides plus, other primitive functions can be used with / to form reductions. For example:

-/B Minus-reduction

×/B Times-reduction

÷/B Divide-reduction

• Power or Exponentiation *A⋆B*

The left argument is raised to the power indicated by the right argument. For example:

```
9*2       nine-squared
¯3*3      negative three-cubed
16*.5     16 to the one-half power or the square root of 16
```

• Maximum *A⌈B*

The larger of the arguments. For example:

```
      8⌈6
8

      3 5 2⌈1 5 6
3 5 6
```

• Minimum *A⌊B*

The lesser of the arguments. For example:

```
      8⌊6
6

      3 5 2⌊1 5 6
1 5 2
```

• Factorial *!B*

The factorial of the argument. For example:

```
      !5
120

      !3 4 5
6 24 120
```

Note: The symbol ! is formed by ' backspace ..

• Negation *-B*

The argument negated. For example:

```
      -5
¯5

      -¯5
5
```

• Reciprocal ÷*B*

The quotient of 1 divided by the argument. For example:

```
      ÷5
0.2

      ÷4   3   2
0.25  0.3333333333  0.5
```

Section 3.6 SOLUTIONS TO THE EXERCISES

(Expressions for deriving numeric results are given.)

1. b. ⍴*BOB*

   ⍴*CAROL*

   ⍴*TED*

   ⍴*ALICE*

   c. ⍴*BOB*,*CAROL*,*TED*,*ALICE*

   d. *MEAN BOB*

   MEAN CAROL

   MEAN TED

   MEAN ALICE

   e. *HCAP BOB*

   HCAP CAROL

   HCAP TED

   HCAP ALICE

   f. +/*BOB*

   +/*CAROL*

   +/*TED*

   +/*ALICE*

   +/*BOB*,*CAROL*,*TED*,*ALICE*

   g. *MEAN BOB*,*CAROL*,*TED*,*ALICE*

2.
```
     ∇Q←B HCAP A
[1]    Q←.75×B-MEAN A
     ∇
```

3. See summary

4. *DIFFERENCE* find the difference between each element in the input vector and the average of the elements in the vector.

5. Reduction reduces the elements of the vector into a single number. Catenation does not reduce. Try:

✓ 2, ¯6, 10

6. a. `24÷+/7 3 ¯5`

   b. `16+×/5 2 ¯11 3`

7. Dyadic function ⌈ (called maximum) finds the maximum of its arguments. Line 1 of function *SUPER* says a bowler whose average is over 200 has a handicap of zero. The 0⌈....expression assures that the super bowler will not be penalized with a negative handicap. ⌈/ selects the largest element in the vector.

8. a. The function ⌊ (called minimum) finds the minimum of its arguments and ⌊/ selects the smallest element in the vector. Line 1 of the function can be shortened to read `Z←(⌈/X),⌊/X`

   b.
```
     ∇Z←REPORT X
[1]    Z←(MEAN X), (SUPER X), (⍴X), (⌈/X),⌊/X
     ∇
```

   c. `⌈/BOB`

   `⌈/BOB, CAROL, TED, ALICE`

   `⌊/CAROL`

   `CAROL[⍴CAROL]-⌊/CAROL`

9. a.
```
     ∇Z←ABS X
[1]    Z←X⌈-X
     ∇
```

The function *ABS* works on vectors.

b.
```
    ∇Z←AL X
[1]  Z←ABS ⌈/X
    ∇
```

or

```
    ∇Z←AL X
[1]  Z←(⌈/X)⌈-⌈/X
    ∇
```

The monadic primitive function | is the absolute value function. Try it:

```
✓      |3

✓      |¯3

✓      |2.1  ¯3  4.1  ¯5.6
```

10. a. The function works by dividing the difference of the mean of the scores by the absolute value of the difference.

b. In case of a tie, 1 is given. 0÷0 in APL is 1. Any other number divided by zero results in a *DOMAIN ERROR* report.

LESSON 4 BRANCHING

A new concept in programming--branching--is introduced in this lesson. In order to make the concept clear, simple functions are used; however, the techniques employed are valuable and have a wide range of applications.

Section 4.1 THE BRANCH STATEMENT

Sign on, if you have not already done so. Load your workspace and:

```
✓   )COPY __________* LESSONS EX4
```

Execute the monadic function *ROOT* with a positive argument. For example:

```
✓   ROOT 25
✓   ROOT 68
✓   ROOT 100
```

What happens if you enter a negative number? Try it:

```
✓   ROOT ¯25
```

ROOT prints the square root of the argument. Since the square root of a negative number is imaginary, an error occurs if the argument is not a positive number. Type:

```
√    →
```

to wipe out the error and to terminate function execution. Now execute *AROOT*, using the same values you used when you executed *ROOT*:

```
√    AROOT 25
√    AROOT 68
√    AROOT 100
```

AROOT appears to work exactly like *ROOT*. What happens if you enter a negative number? Try it:

```
√    AROOT ¯25
```

No error occurs, but the function stops executing without printing anything. Look at the *ROOT* and *AROOT* functions to see what in the coding makes the difference.

```
√    ∇ROOT[⎕]∇
√    ∇AROOT[⎕]∇
```

As you can see, *AROOT* has an extra line of coding. Line 1 is a decision point. The function at this point will follow one of two paths:

1. Function execution will stop if the argument is negative.
2. Function execution will continue if the argument is positive.

The expression of line 1 is known as a <u>branch statement</u>. Its purpose is to direct the execution of the function by indicating what line of the function should be the next executed. It has three components:

1. A branch symbol, a right pointing arrow, →

2. A directing expression made up of 0 or any positive integer and ×ι

3. A relationship on which the decision to take one path or the other is made

Let us take a close look at the branch statement of line 1 piece by piece as it would be executed from right to left. The parenthesized letters in the diagram refer to the discussion of the parts of the branch statement that follows.

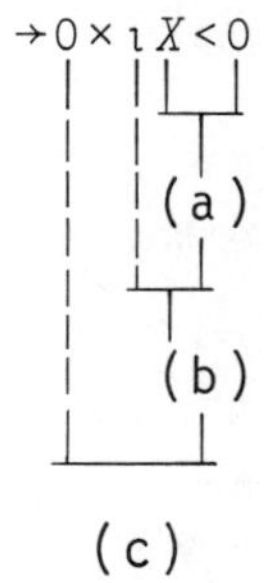

(a) $X<0$

Each of the relational functions < ≤ = ≥ > ≠ results in a 1 if the relationship between the arguments is true or a 0 if the relationship between the arguments is false. Verify this with the following expressions at the terminal:

√	3=3	3=5
√	4≠8	4≠4
√	3<5	3<3
√	5<3	5≤3
√	3≤3	3≤5
√	4≥4	8≥4
√	4≥8	4>8
√	8>4	8>0

A relational function in a branch statement is used to test whether a condition is true or not. The expression $X<0$ will have the value 1 if X is negative, and $X<0$ will have the value 0 if X is zero or positive. You can verify this by typing:

```
✓   X←¯9
✓   X<0
✓   X←5
✓   X<0
```

(b) ⍳X<0

Since the value of $X<0$ can only be 1 or 0, we have two alternatives to consider:

1. What is the value of ⍳1?
2. What is the value of ⍳0?

The value of ⍳1, as you may recall from the definition of ⍳, is 1; that is, the positive integers up to and including 1. (⍳Y results in the positive integers from 1 through Y.)

The expression ⍳0 results in a vector called the <u>empty vector</u>. This is a vector of <u>no</u> components which has special uses. In branching, a branch to the empty vector simply results in the next line of the function being executed. Additional uses of the empty vector are discussed in later lessons. The appearance or representation of the empty vector at the terminal is startling, as you will see if you type:

```
✓   ⍳0
```

What did you see? If you typed the expression correctly, all you saw was a linefeed--no printing. If you use monadic rho, ⍴, with the empty vector, the result will be 0, since the number of components in the empty vector is zero. Try:

```
✓   W←⍳0
✓   W
✓   ⍴W
```

(c) `0×⍳X<0`

From (b) above we know that the value of `⍳X<0` is either `1` or the empty vector. One feature of the empty vector is that anything times the empty vector is still the empty vector. Try:

✓	`4×⍳0`
✓	`¯7×⍳0`
✓	`0×⍳0`

Thus, the entire branch expression `0×⍳X<0` will have either the value `0` (that is, `0×1`) or the empty vector (that is, `0×` the empty vector). If the value of the branch expression is `0`, the next line executed is line `0`, because the argument of the `→` tells which statement to go to next. There is no `0` statement in the function definition--the line number `0` is assigned to the header only for editing purposes, not for execution--and so execution of the function stops after the first line. If the value of the branch expression is the empty vector, execution of the function always continues with the next numbered statement in the function; in this case, statement 2. If there is no next numbered statement, execution of the function stops.

Execution of a function continues line by line until a branch statement is reached. Then execution may be directed to some other line of the function. A two-path branch like the one of the *AROOT* function is very common. Its basic components again are

`→`	statement number	`×⍳`	relationship; which says
go to	statement number	if	relationship is true; continue execution if not true

For example, the expression

```
→6×⍳Y≠44
```

says: go to statement number 6 if the value of *Y* is not equal to `44`; otherwise, continue with the next statement in line.

Another expression that creates a two-path branch where one of the paths is to stop function execution is

```
→statement number × relationship
```

Using this form of branch statement line 1 of *AROOT* would be

```
→2×X≥0
```

That is, go to statement 2 if *X* is positive or equal to zero; otherwise, stop. Note that this form can only be used if one of the paths is to stop function execution. The first form discussed can be used when both paths continue with the function execution.

Two often useful tests that can be made in a branch statement are determining whether a number is an integer and determining whether a number is even. Each test employs a new APL function.

The monadic function ⌊ (called floor) rounds its argument down to the nearest integer. Try:

√	⌊7.9	⌊7.2
√	⌊75.1	⌊6.5
√	⌊3.476	⌊¯3.3
√	⌊¯3.8	⌊9.1 ¯6.7 8.61 4.5 3.83
√	⌊7	⌊¯3

In the last two examples--where the argument was an integer--the result was the same as the argument; that is, for the argument *A*, *A*=⌊*A*. This relationship is true only if *A* is an integer, and so we have a simple means of determining whether a number is an integer. Try:

√	A←3
√	A=⌊A
√	A←3.5
√	A=⌊A

A function analogous to floor is the monadic function ⌈ (called ceiling). Ceiling rounds up to the nearest integer. Test ⌈ with the arguments given for ⌊ above.

Another means of testing for an integer is to use the dyadic function | (called residue). The residue function is most often used as a remainder function. In this case, both arguments are greater than or equal to zero and the left argument is an integer. The result is the remainder after the left argument is divided into the right. Try the following:

✓	3|15	3|14
✓	2|4	6|39
✓	6|48	5|22
✓	1|15	1|13.4

In the last example where the right argument is a fraction, the result is the fractional part. In the next-to-last example where the right argument is an integer, the result is zero. Thus an expression for testing whether *N* is an integer is 0=1|*N*. Try:

```
✓    A←3
✓    0=1|A
✓    A←3.5
✓    0=1|A
```

A number is even if it is divisible by 2 without a remainder; that is, for *N*, 0=2|*N*. This relationship is true only if *N* is an even number. Here, then, is a means of determining whether a number is even. Try:

```
✓    0=2|14
✓    0=2|15
```

How would you determine whether a number was odd?

EXERCISES I

1. For each of the following, determine which line of the function will be executed next after the branch command.

   a. Assume that the value of *N* is 14

   ```
   [3]    →0×ιN>25
   ```

   b. Assume that the value of *I* is 10

   ```
   [5]    →2×ιI≤10
   ```

   c. Assume that the value of *R* is 6

   ```
   [6]    →9×ιR<0
   ```

   d. Assume that the value of *R* is ¯6

   ```
   [6]    →9×ιR<0
   ```

   e. Assume that the value of *T* is 3 5 7 3

   ```
   [8]    →0×ι10≥ρT
   ```

   f. Assume that the value of *J* is 8

   ```
   [4]    →7×1=2|J
   ```

   g. Assume that the value of *J* is 5

   ```
   [4]    →7×1=2|J
   ```

2. Write expressions for the variable *SP* to determine whether

   a. *SP* is less than 100

   b. *SP* is not equal to zero

   c. *SP* is greater than or equal to *AG*

   d. *SP* is positive

   e. The number of components in the vector *SP* is equal to 12

3. Construct branch statements for the following:

   a. Go to statement 6 if *TP* is negative; if not, go to the next statement.

   b. Go to statement 3 if *I* is less than or equal to 100; if not, continue.

c. Stop execution if *MIS* has 9 components; otherwise, continue.

4. Define a function *MQR* with header ∇*MQR F* that will print the product of all the components of *F* if the number of components of *F* is less than 5; if not, the function should print nothing. For example, *MQR* 1 2 3 4 will result in 24. *MQR* 9 6 5 4 2 will produce no result.

Section 4.2 EFFECT OF HAVING EXPLICIT RESULT IN A FUNCTION WITH BRANCHING

If you look once again at the headers of the *ROOT* and *AROOT* functions--∇*ROOT X* and ∇*AROOT X*--you will see that they are functions without explicit results, and indeed, the statement *X*⋆.5 in the functions is a print statement. As you saw in Lesson 3, a function without an explicit result has limited use. The function *BROOT* is identical to *AROOT* except that it has an explicit result. Look at it.

```
∇BROOT[⎕]∇
```

Test the function.

```
BROOT 25

3×BROOT 25

BROOT ¯25

3×BROOT ¯25
```

An error occurred in the last statement because execution of *BROOT* ended before a result had been assigned to *Z*, yet the expression 3×*BROOT* ¯25 needs a result.

To avoid an error report when defining a function with an explicit result, it is necessary to assign a value to the explicit result before any branch statement that might halt execution of the function. Sometimes this creates a problem. In *BROOT*, for example, what could we use as a value for *Z* before the function has determined whether the argument is valid? Remembering that ⍳0 gives a blank line, we could use ⍳0 as an initial value for *Z*. If *X* is positive, the proper value of *Z* will be specified later in the execution; if *X* is negative, the result will be ⍳0. For example, edit *BROOT* as follows:

```
√    ∇BROOT[.1]Z←⍳0∇
```

Then display it:

```
√    ∇BROOT[⎕]∇
```

Now try the following:

```
√    BROOT ¯25
√    3×BROOT ¯25
√    3×BROOT 25
```

In problems like this, it is up to the programmer or the user of the function to determine whether an artificial result, like ⍳0, suits his needs better than an error report.

When the result of a function depends on the type of argument that is entered, it is usually possible to specify the result to meet one condition before the branch test is made. For example, the function *NON* is a monadic function with an explicit result. Test the function:

```
√    NON ¯3
√    2×NON ¯3
√    NON 7
√    3×NON 7
```

The result is the argument if it is zero or positive and the result is the square of the argument if it is negative. Study the definition:

```
√    ∇NON[⎕]∇
```

EXERCISES II

5. Define a function with header ∇*Z*←*ABS T* as follows: if *T* is positive or zero, the result is *T*; if *T* is negative, the result is -*T*.

6. Define a function with header ∇*Q*←*PRT M* as follows: If *M* is not an integer, the result is the fractional part; if *M* is an integer, the result is ¯1.

7. Define a function with header ∇*S*←*TRS B* as follows: If *B* has an odd number of components, the result is the odd components of *B*. If *B* has an even number of components, the result is the even components of *B*. For example, *TRS* 11 17 13 14 15 should give the first, third, and fifth elements of the vector, because there are an odd number of elements in the vector; the result should be 11 13 15. *TRS* 22 23 24 25 should give the even components, the second and fourth, since there are an even number of components in the vector; the result is 23 25.

Section 4.3 TRACING THE EXECUTION OF A FUNCTION

In the functions that have been shown so far, one path that might be taken has always been to halt function definition; the other path was to execute the next statement. Here is a problem that requires two different solutions:

> Define a function with header ∇*Z*←*FN X* whose argument is a vector. If *X* has an even number of components, the result is the average of the middle two components. If *X* has an odd number of components, the result is the middle component.

A first pass at defining the function might look like this:

```
      ∇Z←FN X
[1]    →3×⍳0=2|⍴X
[2]    Z←X[⌈.5×⍴X]
[3]    Z←.5×X[.5×⍴X]+X[1+.5×⍴X]
    ∇
```

This definition was copied into your workspace with the group *EX4*. Try it out:

```
✓        FN 4 9 6 3

✓        FN 4 9 6 3 7
```

What happened? With an odd number of components, statement 2 should have been executed, but the error report shows statement 3 was tried. Let us trace the execution of the function. Type:

✓ →

✓ TΔFN←1 2 3

TΔ with the function name sets up a <u>trace vector</u>. The vector of numbers to the right of the specification are statement numbers. During the execution of the function, the values of the expressions on the lines indicated in the trace vector will be typed out. If you execute:

```
FN 4 9 6 3 7
```

The printout will look like this:

```
FN[1]
FN[2]  6
FN[3]  DOMAIN ERROR
FN[3]  Z←0.5×X[0.5×ρX]+X[1+0.5×ρX]
                       ^
```

The trace on a function is stopped by typing:

```
TΔFN←ι0
```

Now to find out what happened. You can see from the trace that statement 2 was executed, as expected. But so was statement 3, and that is not what was wanted. What is needed is to stop execution of the function after statement 2, whenever statement 2 is executed. This can be done with an <u>unconditional branch</u>

```
→0
```

placed between statements 2 and 3. Whenever this unconditional branch is executed, the outcome will be a halt to function execution. <u>Edit</u> *FN* by reentering definition mode:

✓ ∇FN

The computer responds with the next statement number, [4]. Since you want to make an insertion between [2] and [3], override the [4] with [2.1]. The completed line, with the [4] typed by the computer and the rest typed by you, looks like:

✓ [4] [2.1] →0

The computer responds with [2.2]. Since there is nothing more to insert, close definition with a del, ∇.

```
✓   [2.2] ∇
```

Every time function definition is closed, the statements are put in order and renumbered as consecutive integers. Verify this for the edited function *FN* by entering:

```
✓   ∇FN[⎕]∇
```

Now try the edited function.

```
✓   FN 4 9 6 3 7
```

And, to be safe, try

```
✓   FN 4 9 6 3
```

Now what? The even components were working before. Why not now? We can, if we wish, once again trace the execution of the function. Or we can examine the printout of the definition to see whether we can locate the problem. The first statement of *FN* says branch to statement 3 if *X* has an even number of components. But statement 3, since we made the insertion, is no longer `Z←.5×X[.5×ρX]+X[1+.5×ρX]`, it is `→0`. Statement 1 is no longer correct for this function.

✓ Statement 1 will have to be edited to `→4×ι0=2|ρX`. Do it and try the function again.

Section 4.4 LABELS

Insertions, such as that done to *FN* in Sec. 4.3, deletions, and other changes to a function definition occur frequently. Instead of editing branch statements each time the line numbering sequence changes and affects the branching, it is possible to branch to a label, a name associated with a statement, rather than to a statement number. A label is a variable; it precedes the statement and is separated from it by a colon. For example, statement 4 of *FN* with a label looks like this:

✓
```
[4]   EVEN: Z←.5×X[.5×ρX]+X[1+.5×ρX]
```

Edit your function to branch to a label. The revised function should look like this:

```
      ∇Z←FN X
[1]   →EVEN×⍳0=2|ρX
[2]   Z←X[⌈.5×ρX]
[3]   →0
[4]   EVEN: Z←.5×X[.5×ρX]+X[1+.5×ρX]
  ∇
```

Now changes to the function definition will not affect the branching sequence. For example, suppose that the function is meant to work on the magnitude of the components of *X*. Then the first step of the function would be to take the absolute value of *X*. The absolute value is a monadic function represented by |, |*A*. Insert a statement before statement 1 of *FN* respecifying *X* to be |*X*:

✓
```
∇FN[.1]X←|X∇
```

Display the edited function by typing:

✓
```
∇FN[⎕]∇
```

and test the function to be certain that it still works properly:

✓ ✓ ✓ ✓
```
FN 4 9 6 3
FN 4 9 6 3 7
FN ¯5 6 ¯4 ¯7 ¯5
FN ¯1 ¯6 4 7
```

With labeled statements there is no need to edit the branch statements when the numbering sequence changes.

EXERCISES III

8. A manufacturer gives a 1.5% discount to its customers if they pay their bills on or before the tenth of the month. Define a function *DIS* with header *∇DUE←DAY DIS BILL* to reflect the amount due given the day of the month and the gross bill. Test your function by executing the following commands and any others you desire:

```
14 DIS 32.45
8  DIS 46.98
```

9. Suppose the brokerage fee on round lot (in groups of 100) stock purchases of two ranges of stock are:

Cost per share	Fee
\$0 - \$24.99	1% plus \$7
\$25 - \$50	0.5% plus \$19

Define a function *FEE* with header *∇PAY←COST FEE LOTS*, where *COST* is the cost paid per share and *LOTS* is the number of lots, to determine the brokerage fee paid. If the cost per share is greater than \$50, the function execution should terminate.

Test your function by executing the following commands and any others you desire:

```
32 FEE 4
65 FEE 7
12 FEE 19
```

10. A chemical firm prepares a mix of three ingredients with the following costs:

Ingredient	Cost per pound for purchases of 1000 pounds or less	Cost per pound for purchases over 1000 pounds
A	\$.21	\$.19
B	.15	.13
C	.07	.06

Additional cost is \$.63 for each 35 pound bag. Partially filled bags are charged for. Prices above are based on the total weight of the mix.

Define a function *COST* with header ∇*Z*←*PERCENT COST WT*, where *PERCENT* is a vector of percentages of the three ingredients in the mix and *WT* is the total weight desired, to determine the total cost of the order. Test your function by executing the following commands and any others you may desire.

```
15 30 55 COST 1700
20 5 75 COST 350
0 50 50 COST 3400
```

Section 4.5 SUMMARY

Branching. There are two types of branching--conditional and unconditional branching. An unconditional branch command has two parts:

(1)	(2)
go to	statement number or label name
Example: →	*LAB*

A conditional branch has four parts:

	(1)	(2)	(3)	(4)	
	go to	statement # or label name	if	a relationship is true	
Example:	→	*A*	×⍳	5=*B*	(→*A*×⍳5=*B*)
Example:	→	*A*	×	5=*B*	(→*A*×5=*B*)

The expression ⍳0 represents the empty vector, a vector of no components. If the value of the expression in a branch command is ⍳0, the execution of the function continues with the next numbered statement. If the value of the expression in a branch command is 0, the execution of the function terminates. If the value of the expression in a branch command is a statement number of the function, that statement number is the next executed.

Labels. A label can be used as a variable for a statement number in a branch command. The label is given the value of the current statement number of the statement to which it is attached. The form for a labeled statement is:

[statement number] label: contents of the statement

A defined function whose syntax includes an explicit result should have the explicit result assigned a value within the function definition.

Function Editing. A useful means of following the execution of a function is a function trace. As execution of the function progresses, the results of any statements whose statement number appears in the trace vector will be printed. To initiate a trace, the trace vector *T∆NAME* is assigned statement numbers to trace. *NAME* is the name of the function. For example, *T∆GO*←1 3 7 causes the results of statements 1, 3, and 7 of function *GO* to be printed. The next and all subsequent executions of the function are traced. Tracing can be discontinued by specifying the trace vector to be the empty vector, for example, *T∆GO*←⍳0 discontinues the trace of *GO*.

A line can be inserted in a function definition by using decimal statement numbers. For example, [4.6] causes an insertion between statements 4 and 5. When function definition is closed, the statements are renumbered as consecutive integers, and the labels are respecified with values equal to the current statement number of the statement with which they are associated.

Section 4.6 SOLUTIONS TO THE EXERCISES

1. a. 4 b. 2

   c. 7 d. 9

   e. 0 f. 0

   g. 7

2. a. *SP*<100 b. *SP*≠0

   c. *SP*≥*AG* d. *SP*>0

   e. 12=⍴*TX*

3. a. →6×⍳*TP*<0 b. →3×⍳*I*≤100 c. →0×⍳9=⍴*MIS*

4.
```
    ∇MQR F
[1]   →0×⍳5≤⍴F
[2]   ×/F
    ∇
```

5.
```
    ∇Z←ABS T
[1]    Z←T
[2]    →0×⍳T≥0
[3]    Z←-T
    ∇
```

6.
```
    ∇Q←PRT M
[1]    Q←¯1
[2]    →0×⍳M=⌊M
[3]    Q←M-⌊M
    ∇
```

7.
```
    ∇S←TRS B
[1]    S←B[¯1+2×⍳⌈.5×⍴B]
[2]    →0×⍳1-2|⍴B
[3]    S←B[2×-.5×⍴B]
    ∇
```

8.
```
    ∇DUE←DAY DIS BILL
[1]    DUE←BILL
[2]    →0×⍳DAY>10
[3]    DUE←.985×DUE
    ∇
```

```
92.45
46.2753
```

Note: If your answers check, your function is probably correct, even if not identical to the ones shown.

9.
```
    ∇PAY←COST FEE LOTS
[1]    →0×⍳COST>50
[2]    →F1×⍳COST≥25
[3]    PAY←LOTS×7+.01×100×COST
[4]    →0
[5]    F1: PAY←LOTS×19+.005×100×COST ∇
```

```
140
no result
361
```

See note to problem 8 above.

10.
```
    ∇Z←PERCENT COST WT
[1]    AC←.63×⌈WT÷35
[2]    →C1×⍳WT>1000
[3]    Z←AC+WT×.01×+/PERCENT×.21  .15  .07
[4]    →0
[5]    C1:  Z←AC+WT×.01×+/PERCENT×.19  .13  .06
    ∇
```

```
201.72
42
384.74
```

See note to problem 8 above.

LESSON **5**

ITERATIVE FUNCTIONS, CONVERSATIONAL FUNCTIONS, AND CHARACTER HANDLING

Lesson 5 continues the discussion of defining functions by introducing more techniques for processing the input data.

Section 5.1 AN ITERATIVE FUNCTION

Here is a problem whose solution requires repeating certain steps several times. Suppose you are given a list of numbers --say, 92 ¯12 17 26 31 ¯56 9--to sort in ascending order. How might you do it? One way is to scan the list for the lowest number. Write it down in a new list and remove it from the old list:

```
New list:  ¯56
Old list:  92  ¯12  17  26  31  9
```

Then repeat the process until the old list has no more numbers in it:

```
New list:  ¯56  ¯12
Old list:  92  17  26  31  9
New list:  ¯56  ¯12  9
Old list:  92  17  26  31
```

And so on.

This procedure or <u>algorithm</u> is well-defined. It has a definite beginning, a number of steps to follow, and a means of determining when to stop. A program to sort a list of numbers can be written using this algorithm. What do we need?

1. The original list to be sorted. Let's call it *OL* for <u>o</u>riginal <u>l</u>ist.

2. A new list to be built up with the sorted numbers. Let's call it *NL*.

3. A means of finding the lowest number in *OL*. Recall the expression ⌊/*OL* (discussed in Lesson 3) will do this.

4. A means of adding the components selected from *OL* to *NL*. We have catenation.

5. A means of eliminating a component from *OL*. Doing this requires a new APL primitive function called <u>compression</u>. Compression is a dyadic function whose left and right arguments are vectors of the same length. The left argument must be composed only of zeros and/or ones. The right argument can be any vector. The result is only those components of the right argument whose corresponding components in the left argument are ones. For example:

```
      1  0  1  0/2  4  6  8
```

selects the first and third components or 2 6 from the right argument. Try also:

```
√    0  1  1  1  0/9  ¯13  15  8  6

√    0  1  0  1  0  1/ι6

√    1  1  1  1/3  9  8  5

√    1/3  9  8  5

√    0  0  0  0/3  9  8  5

√    0/3  9  8  5

√    T←14  ¯13  18  ¯65  ¯6  10

√    T<0

√    (T<0)/T
```

In the third and fourth examples, all the components are selected. In the fifth and sixth examples, no components are selected and the result is the empty vector. In the last example, the left argument is an expression using a relationship that produces zeros and ones. It is such a relationship that will be used to eliminate the lowest number from the original list in the sort program. Try the following with the *T* specified above:

```
✓   ⌊/T

✓   T≠⌊/T

✓   T←(T≠⌊/T)/T

✓   T
```

Notice that ¯65 is missing from the result. Now try again:

```
✓   T←(T≠⌊/T)/T

✓   T
```

Now ¯13 is also missing.

Finally we need:

6\. A means of repeating the process until no components exist in *OL*. For this we have <u>conditional branching</u>. We want to repeat as long as there are components in *OL* or as long as ⍴*OL* is not 0. The statement

```
      →L1×⍳0≠⍴OL
```

where *L*1 is a label does this.

Once the procedure has been established--that is, once you have an idea of how to do what you want done--function definition can begin by entering definition mode and establishing a function header:

```
      ∇NL←SORT OL
```

The header shows *NL* as the result, the function name as *SORT*, and the argument as *OL*.

Coding the solution as we have stated it in words might produce the following definition.

Add the lowest number in the old list to the new list:

```
[1]   L1:  NL←NL,⌊/OL
```

Remove the lowest number from the old list:

```
[2]   OL←(OL≠⌊/OL)/OL
```

Repeat the process until there are no more components in the old list:

```
[3]   →L1×ι0≠ρOL ∇
```

The function *SORT* as it is defined above is in the workspace *LESSONS*. Copy it into your workspace:

```
√     )COPY ____________* LESSONS SORT
```

Then examine its definition:

```
√     ∇SORT[⎕]∇
```

Now we can specify a test vector and execute the function immediately to see if it works or we can "desk check" it--work it out by hand. Let us follow the first course:

```
√     TEST←92  9  17  26  31  ¯56  ¯12

√     SORT TEST
```

The execution of the function does not continue for long. A value error occurs right at line 1. At the start of function execution, there has been no *NL* variable specified. We know, however, that to start off, *NL* is an empty list. It has no components. To avoid a value error in the function execution, some initial value needs to be assigned to *NL*. How? Here is another use of the <u>empty</u> <u>vector</u>. *NL* can be specified to be ι0--*NL*←ι0. Then neither a value error nor a damaged sorted list will occur, since *NL*←ι0 specifies *NL* to be a vector of no components. Type:

```
√     →
```

to leave function execution. Now edit *SORT* so that the first statement is *NL*←ι0:

```
√     ∇SORT[.1]NL←ι0∇
```

And look at the corrected function:

✓
```
∇SORT[⎕]∇
```

Is the branch statement still all right? The label has stayed with the proper statement. *SORT* should work. Try it:

✓
```
SORT TEST
```

Try again with:

```
✓  M←9 6 ¯3 9 19 ¯4 18 ¯3
✓  SORT M
```

A result was given, but is it the one you expected? The result, as you can see, does not show the duplicates. Something is wrong with the way the new list is being composed. In fact, that fault can be traced back to the prose description of the procedure. Notice that the thinking implicit there is that there is a single lowest number. What we should have said at step 3 is that we need a means of finding all occurrences of the lowest number in *OL*. The new list is composed at line 2, where the smallest value in *OL* is catenated to *NL*. The function ⌊/ (minimum-reduction) gives a scalar result even when there are two or more "smallest" elements in the vector. For example, try:

✓
```
⌊/3 5 3 8 9 3
```

We can use compression, however, to select all the occurrences of the lowest number in *OL* with the expression (*OL*=⌊/*OL*)/*OL*. Do you see how it works? Try:

```
✓  T←9 3 8 3 6
✓  T=⌊/T
✓  (T=⌊/T)/T
```

Edit *SORT* so that line 2 is:

✓
```
[2]   L1:NL←NL,(OL=⌊/OL)/OL
```

Now test *SORT* on *M*:

```
✓   SORT M
```

It works. Does *SORT* still work if the argument has no duplicates? Try:

```
✓   SORT TEST
```

Now the function *SORT* sorts the complete list of numbers in ascending order.

SORT can be used to sort numbers in descending order also, by negating the argument and then the result. For instance, try:

```
✓   -SORT -TEST

✓   -SORT -M
```

EXERCISES I

1. Write expressions, using compression, for the following:

   a. The components in the vector *R* that are even numbers.

   b. The components in the vector *S* that are odd numbers.

   c. All the components in the vector *V* that are even numbers, followed by all the components that are odd numbers.

   d. The factors of a number *N*.

   e. All components that are integers in the vector *M*.

   f. All components in a vector *SP* that are less than 100.

   g. All components in the vector *TM* that are negative.

   h. All components in the vector *SP* that are greater than or equal to the number *AG*.

2. Define a function with header ∇*Z*←*SCAN V* whose argument is a vector and whose result *Z* is a vector of the same length

as *V*. The *I*th component of *Z* is the sum of the first *I* terms of *V*. If *V* is 6 7 3 2, the result will be:

6, (6+7), (6+7+3), 6+7+3+2, that is, 6 13 16 18

Try your function with:

```
      SCAN 1  3  4  6  5

      SCAN 2  ¯4  6  2
```

and any other arguments you wish.

3. A Fibonacci series is a set of numbers starting with where each successive number is the sum of the last and next-to-last numbers. For example, 1 1 2 3 5 8. Define a function with header ∇*Z*←*FIB N* that produces a Fibonacci series of *N* terms. Try:

```
      FIB 8

      FIB 12
```

and any others that interest you. If you need a hint for finding the last and next-to-last numbers in a vector, turn the page upside down.

4. Compression is used in a statement where a branch to one of two or more locations may occur. For example, the allowance for subsistence in the armed forces in 1969 was determined in one of three ways:

1. When rations in kind were not available, $2.57 per day.
2. When permission to mess separately was granted, $1.32 per day.
3. When assigned to duty under emergency conditions where no government messing facilities were available, $3.42 per day.

The function *SUBSIST* shown below determines the allowance. Inputs to the function are the number of days as a left argument and reason for allowance as the right argument. The right argument is 1, 2, or 3 according to the determinations

---

Hint: Recall that ⍴*X* tells the number of components in the vector *X*. The last index number of *X* is then ⍴*X* and the last component is *X*[⍴*X*].

listed above. Study the branch of line 1:

```
      ∇ALLOW←DAYS SUBSIST TYPE
[1]   →(TYPE=1 2)/S1,S2
[2]   ALLOW←DAYS×3.42
[3]   →0
[4]   S1:ALLOW←DAYS×2.57
[5]   →0
[6]   S2:ALLOW←DAYS×1.32
  ∇
```

Define a function with header ∇*Z←TYPE INT PERIOD* which determines the interest due on a $1000 loan borrowed for a period in months for the following types:

1. Prime commercial, 4 to 6 months, 4.38 per cent per year
2. Prime bankers' acceptance, 90 days, 4.22 per cent per year
3. Call loans, renewal rate, 5.12 per cent per year

(Rates based on 1965 New York City interest rates.) Try your function on the following:

```
      1 INT 5

      2 INT 3

      3 INT 8
```

5. Postal rates vary for each mail class as follows (based on 1970 rates):

   Air Mail: 10¢ for each ounce or fraction. Limit 70 ounces.
   First Class: 6¢ for each ounce or fraction. Limit 13 ounces.
   Second Class: 5¢ for first 2 ounces, 1¢ for each additional ounce.
   Third Class: 6¢ for first 2 ounces, 2¢ for each additional ounce. Limit 16 ounces.

Define a function with header ∇*RATE←CL MAIL WGT* to determine the cost of mailing a letter. For *CL* let 0 be air mail; 1, first class; 2, second class; and 3, third class. Let *WGT* be the weight of the letter in ounces. If the letter exceeds the weight limitations, let the result be the empty vector.

Try your function on the following:

```
0 MAIL 4.3

1 MAIL 2.7

2 MAIL 9

3 MAIL 5.1

1 MAIL 16
```

Section 5.2 AN INTERACTIVE FUNCTION

Branching in Lesson 4 was used to direct the function to follow one of two procedures. The branching of the *SORT* function, on the other hand, served a different purpose. It caused lines 2 and 3 to be executed over and over again. A function with such a branch is generally called an iterative function or a looping function. The function *GUESS* that you used but did not examine in Lesson 2 used iterative branching. (If you wish, copy *GUESS* into your workspace and look at it.) Functions, like *GUESS*, which have some interaction between the user and the program during their execution often employ looping. The discussion that follows gives another example of an interactive function.

Suppose you wish to test a grade-school child on the multiplication tables in this way:

1. As an argument to the function you want the table to be tested. For example, if the function is called *MULTIPLY*, you want *MULTIPLY* 8 to mean a test on the table of eights.

2. You want the numbers from 1 through 12 to be presented randomly.

3. You want the student to be able to enter his answer after each problem is presented.

4. You want to keep score.

5. After he has worked 12 problems, you want to tell him his score.

New uses of APL are needed in order to code steps 2, 3, and 5: for step 2 a means of selecting numbers at random is needed; for step 3 a means of interaction between student and function is needed; and for step 5 a means of displaying a message is needed.

Getting random numbers is done with the ? functions. Used monadically, ? (called roll) selects a random integer from 1 through the argument of ?. The argument may be a vector. Try the following:

✓ ?6	?6
✓ ?6	?25
✓ ?20	?6 6 6 6 6 6
✓ ?6 12 25	?4 8 16

Used dyadically, ? (called deal) selects the number of random integers specified by the left argument from the numbers 1 through the right argument, without duplicates. Both arguments must be scalars, and the left argument cannot be greater than the right. Try:

✓ 1?6	3?6
✓ 6?6	10?10

There is a difference between ?6 6 6 6 6 6 and 6?6. In the first case, ? operates on each component of the vector independently, so that there is a possibility that some number or numbers will be repeated. In the second case, the numbers from 1 through 6 are mixed up (permuted). There can be no duplication. Since, for the *MULTIPLY* program, each of the first twelve integers is to be used only once, the expression needed is 12?12. Either random number function is useful for creating test data with little typing. For example:

```
✓ R←25?100
✓ R
✓ SORT R
```

Execution of a function or an expression is halted for input from the keyboard if a quad ⎕ appears to the right of a specification arrow. Whatever is typed in replaces the quad. Try:

```
✓  CA←3×⎕
```

Note: ⎕: is a signal that something should be typed. Type:

```
✓  6
```

then:

```
✓  CA
```

The result is the product of 3 and 6, the number you typed in. Try again:

```
✓  CA←3×⎕
✓  12
✓  CA
```

Using the quad gives us the means of getting the student's answer to each problem as it is presented. The line in the *MULTIPLY* function that does this is *ANS*←⎕, that is, assign whatever is typed in to the variable *ANS*.

Note: If ever a quad is presented and you do not want to continue, simply type → and the expression or function execution will be terminated.

The quad may also appear to the left of a specification arrow in which case it serves as an explicit command to display the value of the expression to the right of the arrow. It is often used for displaying a variable as well as specifying it. For example, try:

```
✓  ⎕←56×7
✓  56×7
✓  D←56×7
✓  D
✓  ⎕←D←56×7
```

A message in APL is given by enclosing the text--this can be any combination of letters, symbols, and numbers--in single quotes. For example, type:

```
√       'YOUR SCORE WAS'
```

The result is the text just as it was typed, excluding the enclosing quotes. Also try:

```
√       'OH NO'
√       '*○↑↓∇Δ'
√       '9×6+7'
√       'GOOD GRIEF'
```

If the text contains a quote, it must be entered as a double quote. Type:

```
√       'DON''T STOP'
√       'IT AIN''T SO'
```

<u>Warning</u>: If, after entering text, the computer no longer appears to work, try entering another quote and pressing RETURN, before asking for help or assuming that your terminal or the computer is broken. A general rule is that calculations will not be performed unless the number of quotes entered is even.

Let us now examine the predefined function *MULTIPLY*. Copy it into your workspace:

```
√       )COPY ____________* LESSONS MULTIPLY
```

Try using it, if you wish, to test yourself on multiplication by twelve:

```
√       MULTIPLY 12
```

Otherwise, examine the definition:

✓ ∇*MULTIPLY*[⎕]∇

The following commentary describes what occurs as various lines of the function are executed:

Line 1 is an instruction message; it prints out each time the function is executed.

Line 2 mixes up the numbers from 1 through 12 and stores them in *N*.

Line 3 initializes the score counter *SC*. At the start of the function the score is zero. Line 7 adds 1 to the score if the answer typed was correct.

Line 4 initializes a counter *I* to keep track of the number of problems worked. *I* is used in line 5 to present the next component of *N*.

Line 8 increments the counter *I* for the next problem.

Line 9 determines whether more problems are to be presented.

Lines 10 and 11 tell the student his score.

Look at the function header again:

```
∇MULTIPLY X; SC;I;ANS;N
```

It contains the names of the variables used for keeping score (*SC*), for keeping track of the problems presented (*I*), for storing the student answer (*ANS*), and the problem order (*N*), each separated from the header name and argument by a semicolon. This header format establishes each of the variables listed--*SC*, *I*, *ANS*, *N*--as local variables, that is, as variables significant to the function only during execution. After execution of the function, the values of *SC*, *I*, *ANS*, and *N* are not present in the workspace and these variable names do not appear in the)*VARS* list. Any variable whose value is not needed after function execution can be a local variable. The name of each local variable in the function header is preceded by a semicolon.

It is possible to refine the message of lines 10 and 11 of the function *MULTIPLY* so that it appears on one line. To do so requires that character data be intermixed with numeric data. This is done by separating the character part from the numeric part by a semicolon:

```
√       'YOUR SCORE IS ';⌊100×5÷12
```

If you want a space to appear between the text and the numeric value, the space must be part of the text. Try:

```
√       'THE PRODUCT IS'; 9×8

√       'THE PRODUCT IS '; 9×8
```

Edit *MULTIPLY* so that line 10 reads:

```
√   [10] 'YOUR SCORE IS ';⌊100×SC÷12
```

and <u>delete</u> line 11. Deleting is done by pressing the interrupt key on the terminal (this is variously labeled on terminals as ATTN, INDEX, LINEFEED, or INT) and then the RETURN key. When deleting a line, nothing but the interrupt-RETURN sequence can be entered.

The mixed form of character and numeric output can also be used to insert a times sign in the presentation of the problem. Try:

```
√       6;'×';7
```

Edit line 5 of *MULTIPLY* to be:

```
√   [5]  M1:N[I];'×';X
```

Once editing is done, execute the function, noting the messages printed and the requests for input. Look at the function's listing, and follow the execution and the branching. This will help you to see how each step works. If you encounter any difficulty, you may wish to trace the function's execution. (Tracing is done by *T∆MULTIPLY*←line numbers to trace, then executing the function.)

EXERCISES II

6. Modify *MULTIPLY* so that the student will be told what problems he missed, as well as his score.

7. The discriminant $B^2 - 4AC$ of a quadratic equation $AX^2 + BX + C = 0$ tells something about the roots of the equation:

If the discriminant is positive, the roots are real and unequal.
If the discriminant is negative, the roots are imaginary and unequal.
If the discriminant is zero. the roots are real and equal.

Define a function with header ∇*DISC C* to tell (by giving an appropriate message) about the roots of a quadratic equation whose coefficients are the vector *C*.

8. Define a set of two functions to play a simple game of dice. The rules for the main function with header ∇*DICE* are

a. Play continues unless the player types *STOP*. (*STOP* is a variable specified in the function to be 99999.) After the player types *STOP*, the function tells him his score.

b. A player plays by typing *ROLL* when the quad ⎕: appears. *ROLL* is a function with header ∇*D*←*ROLL* which selects two random numbers, each from 1 through 6 to simulate the throwing of the dice.

c. The player should see the results of each roll.

d. Rules of play: On the first roll, player wins if sum of dice is 7 or 11; he loses if sum of dice is 2, 3, or 12. For all other sums, he is told his point (the sum on the dice) and he rolls again. On all rolls but the first, player loses on 7; he wins if the sum equals the sum thrown on the first roll. Otherwise he rolls again.

e. Keep score by adding 1 for each win and subtracting 1 for each loss.

Section 5.3 CHARACTER VECTORS AND FUNCTIONS THAT OPERATE ON THEM

A message, such as that used on line 1 of the *MULTIPLY* function, is just one use of the character vector. Character vectors and numeric vectors are the two types of data vectors available in APL. A character vector is any string of characters enclosed by single quotes. (A single character behaves like a scalar.) A character vector (or scalar) can be assigned to a variable. The value of the variable is the string of characters itself. Try:

```
√    TRS←'TESTING'
√    TRS
√    )VARS
```

Each character in the vector is a component of the vector. This includes spaces, punctuation, and carrier returns. Try:

```
√      ρTRS
√      SST←'ONE TWO'
√      SST
√      ρSST
√      MR←'      '
√      MR
√      ρMR
√      Q←'ONE        (RETURN)
 TWO'
√      Q
√      ρQ
√      Q[4]
√      N←'WHO KNOWS?'
√      N
√      ρN
√      R←'CAN''T TELL'
√      R
√      ρR
```

A character vector can be indexed in the same way as a numeric vector. Try:

```
✓   ALPHA←'ABCDEFGHIJKLMNOPQRSTUVWXYZ'
✓   ALPHA[3 1 2]
✓   ALPHA[10 21 13 16]
✓   ALPHA[2×⍳13]
```

Although ⍴ and indexing are functions that work for character vectors as well as numeric vectors, there are several primitive functions that do not operate on character vectors--the arithmetic functions for example. However, any function that will operate on character vectors will also operate on numeric vectors. In this section we discuss other primitive functions that operate on character vectors (and so, too, on numeric vectors).

Catenation works for character vectors as well as numeric vectors. For example, try:

```
✓   A←'STRAW'
✓   B←'BOSS'
✓   C←'BERRY'
✓   A,B
✓   A,C
✓   'BLUE',C
✓   A,'MAN'
```

Of the relational functions, only = and ≠ can be used with character vectors. Try:

```
✓   'A'='ANAGRAM'
✓   'A'≠'ANAGRAM'
```

```
√   'WEAK'='WEEK'

√   'EARTH'≠'EARLY'

√   'AEIOU'='CURIOUS'
```

On the last example, a length error was indicated because the two character vectors did not have the same number of components. The question that the expression *'AEIOU'= 'CURIOUS'* may have intended to answer is "which vowels are present in the word curious." When presence or nonpresence of an element is all we are interested in, we can use the function ∊, called membership. There is no length conformability requirement for the arguments of ∊. Try:

```
√   'AEIOU'∊'CURIOUS'
```

The result is a 1 for each member of the left argument which is present, somewhere, at least once, in the right argument.

The expression *'AEIOU'∊'CURIOUS'* combined with compression can answer the question "which vowels are present in curious." Try:

```
√   ('AEIOU'∊'CURIOUS')/'AEIOU'
```

The expression *'AEIOU'∊'CURIOUS'* combined with sum-reduction +/ can answer the question "how many different vowels are there in curious."

```
√   +/'AEIOU'∊'CURIOUS'
```

The expression

```
√   +/'CURIOUS'∊'AEIOU'
```

answers the question "how many vowels are there in curious, including duplicates."

Another reduction that is often used with expressions containing character vectors is and-reduction ∧/. If we want to determine if two character vectors *A* and *B* are equal--character for character--we would type ∧/*A*=*B*. Try:

```
✓   A←'BARE'
✓   B←'BEAR'
✓   C←'BARE'
✓   ∧/A=B
✓   ∧/A=C
✓   ∧/B=C
```

And ∧ is a function that operates on ones and zeros. The result of *A*∧*B* is one only if both *A* and *B* are both one; otherwise the result is zero. Or ∨ is another function that operates on only ones and zeros. The result of *A*∨*B* is 0 only if both *A* and *B* are zero; otherwise the result is 1.

A function that has frequent use in combination with the relationals or membership is the monadic function <u>not</u>, ~. Like <u>and</u> and <u>or</u>, the argument of ~ can be only 0 or 1. The result of ~0 is 1 and the result of ~1 is 0. (And, or, and not are often called <u>logic functions</u>.)

Two other functions that are often used when manipulating character data are <u>reversal</u> and <u>rotation</u>. Reversal is a monadic function represented by the symbol ⌽ formed by ○ backspace |. The result is the argument in reverse order. Try:

```
✓   ⌽'TRAP'
✓   ⌽9 8 6 5 3
```

Rotation is a dyadic function represented by the symbol ⌽. The result is the components of the right argument rotated as indicated by the left argument. If the left argument is a positive integer, the rotation is to the left; if the left argument is a negative integer, the rotation is to the right. For example, a left argument of 3 will rotate the first three elements to the end of the vector; a left argument of ¯3 will rotate the last three elements to the front of the vector.

Try:

```
✓   3↑'PLANNING'
✓   ¯3↑'PLANNING'
✓   4↑9  8  2  ¯6  3  4  7
✓   ¯4↑9  8  2  ¯6  3  4  7
```

EXERCISES III

9. Assume:

```
ALP←'ABCDEFGHIJKLMNOPQRSTUVWXYZ'
SYM←'○*ρΔ⎕'
```

Write expressions containing at least one primitive function that will give the following:

a. The twelfth letter of the alphabet.

b. The sixth through the twelfth letters of the alphabet.

c. A random mixing up of the letters of the alphabet.

d. 10 random letters out of the alphabet with no repeats.

e. 10 random letters out of the alphabet with a possibility of repeats.

f. Determining whether the symbol ~ is in *SYM*.

g. Determining whether the symbols ∘Δ∇ are in *SYM*.

h. String *ALP* and *SYM* together into one longer vector.

i. The alphabet in reverse order.

j. The number of o's in the word onomatopoeia.

k. The symbols ρΔ⎕○*.

l. The symbols Δ⎕○*ρ.

m. The index numbers of all the vowels in the alphabet.

At the terminal, specify the variables *ALP* and *SYM* as above.

Then enter each expression, check the results, and modify whe where necessary.

10. Define a function with header ∇*COUNT F* which will count the number of vowels in the character vector *F* and will list the vowel name and the number of occurrences of that vowel. For example:

```
      COUNT 'SHE SELLS SEASHELLS BY THE SEASHORE'
A  2
E  7
I  0
O  1
U  0
```

To test your function, try:

```
      COUNT 'UNITED NATIONS'
```

11. A perfect palindrome is an expression that reads the same forward and backward. The word OTTO is an example. Also, the expression "able was I ere I saw Elba." An imperfect palindrome is an expression that reads the same forward and backward if you disregard spaces and punctuation. For example, the expression "madam, I'm Adam." Define a function with header ∇*Z←PAL X* which will result in a 1 if the character vector *X* is an imperfect or perfect palindrome and a 0 if it is not. Test your function by executing:

```
      PAL 'LIVE NOT ON EVIL'

      PAL 'NOON'

      PAL 'A MAN, A PLAN, A CANAL--PANAMA'

      PAL 'NO MORE MEN'
```

12. A Super Challenge!

Problem 5 of this lesson can be solved using no branching. Can you define a function that will do it?

Section 5.4 SUMMARY

New APL Primitive Functions. The primitive functions introduced in Lesson 5 are defined below.

• Compression *A/B*

A is a vector of 1's and 0's. *B* is a vector of the same length as *A*. The result is all those components of *B* corresponding to 1's in *A*. For example:

```
      1 0 1 0/3 7 6 2
3 6

      1 1 0 0/'ABCD'
AB
```

Compression is often used in a branch statement, especially for a two-way or more branch. For example:

```
      [4]   →((Z>0),Z<0)/LAB1,LAB2
```

If *Z* is positive, the statement labeled *LAB*1 is executed. If *Z* is negative, the statement *LAB*2 is executed; if *Z* is zero, statement 5 is executed.

• Monadic Random (Roll) *?B*

B is a scalar integer or a vector of integers. For each *B*, the result is a number selected randomly from the integers 1 through *B*. For example:

```
      ?5
2

      ?5
5

      ?5
2

      ?5 5 5
4 1 2
```

• Dyadic Random (Deal) *A?B*

Both *A* and *B* must be scalar integers and *A* must not be greater than *B*. The result is a vector of *A* unique integers selected randomly from the integers 1 through *B*. For example:

```
      3?7
4 2 1
```

```
      5?5
1  2  4  5  3

      5?5
5  2  1  4  3
```

• Membership *A*∊*B*

A and *B* can be scalars or vectors. There is no length requirement. The result is a 1 for each component of *A* that is also a component of *B* and a 0 for each component in *A* that is not a component in *B*. For example:

```
      3∊4 3 2
1

      4 3 2∊3
0  1  0

      6 3∊7 2 4.1 6
1  0

      'A'∊'CAT'
1

      'CAT'∊'A'
0  1  0
```

• Not ~*B*

B must be a scalar or vector consisting only of ones and zeros. The result is the complement of *B*. That is, if *B* is 0, the result is 1; if *B* is 1, the result is 0. For example:

```
      ~1 0 1 0
0  1  0  1
```

• Reversal ⌽*B*

The result is the components of *B* in reverse order. For example:

```
      ⌽3 7 6 3 1
1  3  6  7  3

      ⌽'SAW'
WAS
```

• Rotation *A*⌽*B*

A must be an integer. The result is the same as *B* except that the components are rotated *A* positions to the left if *A* is positive and |*A* positions to the right if *A* is negative. For example:

```
      3⌽6 9 4 5 3 2 8
5  3  2  8  6  9  4

      ¯3⌽6 9 4 5 3 2 8
3  2  8  6  9  4  5

      2⌽'PUZZLE'
ZZLEPU

      ¯2⌽'PUZZLE'
LEPUZZ
```

Character Vectors. Character vectors are vectors composed of any keyboard characters, spaces, or returns. A character vector is entered by enclosing the components in single quotes. If a quote is to be a component, it is represented as a double quote ''. A character vector can be assigned to a variable:

```
      P←'PEACH'
```

and indexed:

```
      P[4]
C

      P[4 3 1]
CAP
```

Functions that work with character vectors as well as numeric vectors are equal, not equal, rotation, reversal, membership, catenation, shape, equal-reduction, not equal-reduction, and compression.

Character vectors can be used to give directions or other messages within a function. For example, '*WORK THE FOLLOWING PROBLEMS*'. Character vectors and numeric expressions can be intermixed for display only, by separating the character and numeric parts of the display with semicolons:

```
      'THE AMOUNT IS ';3+4
THE AMOUNT IS 7
```

```
      'IF YOU ANSWERED ';8+X;' YOU WERE WRONG.'
IF YOU ANSWERED 13, YOU WERE WRONG.      (assuming X←5)
```

<u>Input During Function Execution</u>. The use of a quad ⎕ to the right of a specification will cause execution of a function to halt, a ⎕: to be printed, and the keyboard to be released until something is typed to replace the quad. Then execution of the function resumes.

<u>Local Variables</u>. Variables whose values are only important during the execution of a function can be declared <u>local</u> to the function in the function header. This means that once the function has been executed, the local variables cease to exist. Local variables are separated from the function syntax in the header by semicolons. Each local variable is preceded by a semicolon. For example, in

```
      ∇Z←A FUNCT B;I;J;COUNT;RST
```

I, *J*, *COUNT*, and *RST* are all local variables.

Section 5.5 SOLUTIONS TO THE EXERCISES

1. a. `(0=2|R)/R`

   b. `(1=2|S)/S`   `(0≠2|S)/S`

   c. `((0=2|V)/V),(1=2|V)/V`

   d. `(0=(⍳N)|N)/⍳N`

   e. `(M=⌊M)/M`

   f. `(SP<100)/SP`

   g. `(TM<0)/TM`

   h. `(SP≥AG)/SP`

2.
```
      ∇Z←SCAN V
[1]    Z←⍳0
[2]    I←1
[3]    S1:Z←Z,+/V[⍳I]
[4]    I←I+1
[5]    →S1×⍳I≤⍴V
      ∇
```

<u>Note</u>: If your answers to the test vectors were 1 4 8 14 19 and 2 ¯2 4 6, your function probably works even if it is not the same as that shown.

3.
```
      ∇Z←FIB N
[1]    Z←1 1
[2]    I←2
[3]    F1:Z←Z,Z[⍴Z]+Z[¯1+⍴Z]
[4]    I←I+1
[5]    →F1×⍳I<N
      ∇
```

Note: If your answer to *FIB* 8 was 1 1 2 3 5 8 13 21 and to *FIB* 12 was 1 1 2 3 5 8 13 21 34 55 89 144, your function probably works even if it is not the same as that shown.

4.
```
     ∇Z←TYPE INT PERIOD
[1]   R←1000×PERIOD÷12
[2]   →(TYPE=1  2)/R1,R2
[3]   Z←R×.0512
[4]   →0
[5]   R1:Z←R×.0438
[6]   →0
[7]   R2:Z←R×.0422
     ∇
```

Note: If your answers to the test cases were 18.25, 10.55, and 34.133......, your function probably works even if it is not the same as that shown.

5. The function shown below gives the rate in dollars.

```
     ∇RATE←CL MAIL WGT
[1]   →(CL=1 2 3)/FST, SND, TRD
[2]   →M1×⍳WGT>70
[3]   RATE←0.1×⌈WGT
[4]   →0
[5]   FST:→M1×⍳WGT>13
[6]   RATE←0.06×⌈WGT
[7]   →0
[8]   SND:RATE←0.05+0.01×⌈0⌈WGT-2
[9]   →0
[10]  TRD:→M1×⍳WGT>16
[11]  RATE←0.06+0.02×⌈0⌈WGT-2
[12]  →0
[13]  M1:RATE←⍳0
     ∇
```

Note: If your answers to the test cases (in dollars) were .5, .18, .12, .14, and blank line, your function probably works even if it is not the same as that shown.

6. Insert the following lines:

```
[2.1]   RW←⍳0
[7.1]   RW←RW,ANS≠N[I]×X
```

Add the following lines:

```
[12]    →0×⍳0=+/RW      (This line stops execution if all
                          problems are right.)
[13]    'YOU MISSED THE FOLLOWING ';RW/N
```

Note: If your solution is different from the above, check it by executing the altered function, making a few mistakes in multiplying and noting the results.

7.
```
      ∇DISC C;D
  [1]   D←(C[2]*2)-4÷C[1]×C[3]
  [2]   →((D>0),D<0)/UNEQ,IM
  [3]   'ROOTS ARE REAL AND EQUAL'
  [4]   →0
  [5]   UNEQ: 'ROOTS ARE REAL AND UNEQUAL'
  [6]   →0
  [7]   IM: 'ROOTS ARE IMAGINARY'
      ∇
```

Note: As a check on your function, if different from the above:

```
      DISC 1 1 1
ROOTS ARE IMAGINARY

      DISC 1 2 1
ROOTS ARE REAL AND EQUAL

      DISC 1 4 3
ROOTS ARE REAL AND UNEQUAL
```

8.
```
      ∇D←ROLL
  [1]   D←?6 6
      ∇

      ∇DICE;STOP;SC;S;S2
  [1]   STOP←99999
  [2]   SC←0
  [3]   ROLL1:S←⎕
  [4]   →SCORE×⍳STOP=+/S
  [5]   S
  [6]   S←+/S
  [7]   →WIN×⍳+/S=7 11
  [8]   →LOSE×⍳+/S=2 3 12
  [9]   ROLL2:'YOU POINT IS ';S;'; ROLL AGAIN'
  [10]  S2←⎕
  [11]  →SCORE×⍳STOP=+/S2
  [12]  S2
  [13]  S2←+/S2
  [14]  →LOSE×⍳S2=7
  [15]  →WIN×⍳S2=2
  [16]  →ROLL2
  [17]  LOSE:SC←SC-1
  [18]  'YOU LOSE.  ROLL AGAIN'
  [19]  →ROLL1
```

```
[20]  WIN:SC←SC+1
[21]  'YOU WIN.  ROLL AGAIN.'
[22]  →ROLL1
[23]  SCORE:'YOUR SCORE IS ';SC
    ∇
```

Note: If your answer is not the same as that above, execute your functions to see that they satisfy all of the requirements.

9.

a. `ALP[12]`

b. `ALP[5+⍳7]`

c. `ALP[26?26]`

d. `ALP[10?26]`

e. `ALP[?26 26 26 26 26 26 26 26 26 26]`

f. `'~'∊SYM`

g. `'∘Δ∇'∊SYM`

h. `ALP,SYM`

i. `⌽ALP`

j. `+/'O'='ONOMATOPOEIA'`   `+/'ONOMATOPOEIA'∊'O'`

k. `2⌽SYM`   `¯3⌽SYM`

l. `¯2⌽SYM`   `3⌽SYM`

m. `(ALP∊'AEIOU')/⍳26`

10.
```
    ∇COUNT F
[1]   'A   ';+/'A'=F
[2]   'E   ';+/'E'=F
[3]   'I   ';+/'I'=F
[4]   'O   ';+/'O'=F
[5]   'U   ';+/'U'=F
    ∇
```

An alternate solution, using branching, is shown below.

```
     ∇COUNT X;I;V
 [1]   I←1
 [2]   V←'AEIOU'
 [3]   C1:V[I],'    ';+/V[I]=X
 [4]   I←I+1
 [5]   →C1×⍳I≤5
     ∇
```

The results of the test should be as follows, if your function is correct,

```
      COUNT 'UNITED NATIONS'
A   1
E   1
I   2
O   1
U   1
```

11.

```
     ∇Z←PAL X
 [1]   Z←(~X∊' .!;:'',-')/X
 [2]   Z←∧/X=⌽X
     ∇
```

The results of the tests should be:

PAL 'LIVE NOT ON EVIL' should give 1

PAL 'NOON' should give 1

PAL 'A MAN, A PLAN, A CANAL--PANAMA' should give 1

PAL 'NO MORE MEN' should give 0

12.

```
     ∇RATE←CL MAIL WGT
 [1]   WGT←⌈WGT
 [2]   RATE←(⍳(WGT>70 13 1E10 16)[CL+1])×(0 0 0.05 0.06+.1
       .06 .01 .02×0⌈WGT-0 0 2 2)[CL+1]
     ∇
```

The tests should give the same results as in Exercise 5.

LESSON 6 INTRODUCTION TO THE MATRIX

In prior lessons the primary data structure was the vector, a one-dimensional array. This lesson discusses functions for and uses of the matrix, a two-dimensional array.

Section 6.1 THE MATRIX AND GETTING DATA OUT OF IT

A mail-order house sends its customers the following table to help them determine the cost of shipping their orders by parcel post.

lbs \ zone	local	1,2	3	4	5	6	7
1	.50	.60	.60	.65	.70	.80	.85
2	.50	.60	.60	.65	.70	.85	.85
3	.50	.65	.70	.75	.85	.95	1.05
4	.55	.70	.75	.85	.95	1.10	1.20
5	.55	.75	.80	.90	1.05	1.25	1.40
6	.55	.80	.90	1.00	1.15	1.40	1.55
7	.60	.90	.95	1.10	1.30	1.50	1.75
8	.60	.95	1.00	1.15	1.40	1.65	1.90
9	.65	1.00	1.05	1.25	1.50	1.80	2.05
10	.65	1.05	1.15	1.35	1.65	1.90	2.25
11	.65	1.10	1.20	1.40	1.75	2.00	2.40
12	.70	1.15	1.25	1.50	1.85	2.15	2.55
13	.70	1.20	1.35	1.55	1.95	2.25	2.70
14	.75	1.25	1.40	1.65	2.05	2.40	2.85
15	.75	1.30	1.45	1.75	2.15	2.50	3.00

The postal rate, as you can see, is based on the weight of

the order in pounds and the zone, or distance, from the mailing point. So, for example, to find the cost of shipping a five-pound order to the third zone, the purchaser reads across the 5-pound row until he comes to the zone-3 column. In the intersection of the row and column is the cost he is looking for--.80.

A table, like this parcel post table, is a common means of organizing and storing information. The table, unlike the vector--the means of organizing and storing data that we have used in previous lessons--is a rectangular or two-dimensional data array. A two-dimensional array is also known as a <u>matrix</u>. Data is stored in a matrix by <u>row</u> (a horizontal line) and by <u>column</u> (a vertical line). To locate a component in a vector we named its index--its position from the leftmost component. Can we similarly locate a component in a matrix? To answer this question, let us look at the parcel post matrix once again.

Sign on, if you have not done so already, and

✓
```
)COPY ________* LESSONS PPR
```

PPR is the matrix of parcel post rates. It is the body of the table shown above. To see it displayed, type:

```
✓    )DIGITS 3     (to make the matrix print on 8 1/2" wide
✓    PPR                                              paper)
✓    )DIGITS 10    (to return digits display to typical 10)
```

Any number in the matrix occupies both a row and a column. Uniquely identifying its position, then, requires two index numbers--a row index and a column index. The convention followed in APL is that the row index is the first index number and the column index is the second index number. The row and column index numbers are separated by semicolons.

The cost of shipping a 5-pound order to the third zone can be found at *PPR*[5;3]. Type:

✓
```
PPR[5;3]
```

The cost of shipping a 4 or 7 pound order to the fifth zone is:

√ `PPR[4 7;5]`

Notice that the result is a two-component vector. The first component is *PPR*[4;5] and the second component is *PPR*[7;5]. The cost of shipping a 2, 5, 8, or 14 pound order locally or to the fifth or sixth zone is:

√ `PPR[2 5 8 14;1 5 6]`

This time the result is a 4-row by 3-column matrix made up of the components of *PPR* arranged in the following order:

PPR[2;1]	*PPR*[2;5]	*PPR*[2;6]
PPR[5;1]	*PPR*[5;5]	*PPR*[5;6]
PPR[8;1]	*PPR*[8;5]	*PPR*[8;6]
PPR[14;1]	*PPR*[14;5]	*PPR*[14;6]

The cost of shipping a 10-pound order to any zone is *PPR*[10;]. Omitting the column index indicates that all columns are to be included. Type:

√ `PPR[10;]`

The cost of shipping all poundages to the fourth zone is:

√ `PPR[;4]`

Omitting the row index indicates that all rows are to be included. Note that *PPR*[;4] is a vector--arranged horizontally as vectors always are--even though its components form a column of the matrix.

EXERCISES I

1. Write expressions for the following by indexing the matrix *PPR*. Check yourself on the terminal.

   a. A seven pound order to zone 6.

   b. A three or ten pound order to zone 7.

c. A four, six, or twelve pound order to zone 3 or 4.

d. Any order to zone 5.

e. A nine pound order to any zone.

f. The difference in cost between a one pound order shipped locally and a 15 pound order shipped to zone 2.

g. The cost of shipping five orders of eleven pounds each to zone 6.

h. The differences in costs between zones 5 and 7.

Section 6.2 CREATING A MATRIX

The matrix *PPR* was provided for you so that you could practice indexing a matrix without being concerned about how a matrix is created. The most common way that a matrix is formed is by using the dyadic function ⍴ called restructure. To see how it works, type:

```
✓    M←3 4⍴9 7 6 5 2 1 7 4 2 7 8 3
✓    M
```

As you can see, the structure of the result--the number of its rows and columns--is shown in the left argument 3 4. The components that fill up the rows and columns are the components of the right argument taken in order and filling up the matrix row by row.

The structure of the postal rate matrix *PPR* is 15 rows by 7 columns, so the left argument of the expression that created *PPR* was 15 7. The right argument of the expression was a 105 component vector, since 15 x 7 = 105.

There is no requirement that the right argument of ⍴ contain exactly the number of components necessary to fill the matrix. If the right argument has more components than necessary, only those that are necessary are used. For example, try:

```
✓    2 3⍴9 6 5 4 3 2 1 8 4
```

If the right argument has fewer components than necessary, those components are used over again, returning to the beginning after the last is used. Try, for example:

```
✓   2 3⍴9 6 5 4
```

The left argument of the restructure function need not be two numbers. It can be one, two, three, and so forth. Each component of the left argument merely indicates the number of components in a dimension of the resulting array. So, if the left argument is a single number greater than zero, there is only one dimension to the resulting array. An array of one dimension is a vector. For example:

```
✓   9⍴1 2 3
```

The use of restructure to create vectors of repeating components is quite helpful and saves typing. Try:

```
✓   10⍴1 0

✓   5⍴9

✓   ?10⍴10
```

If the left argument of restructure has three components, the result is a third-order array. Similarly, a four-component left argument produces a fourth-order array. All arrays of more than two dimensions are displayed as sets of matrices. In every case, the rightmost two components of the left argument represent the rows and columns of the resulting array. You may wish to see a higher order array. If you do, type:

```
✓   2 3 4⍴24?99
```

While these lessons do not discuss higher order arrays, everything said for matrices applies also to higher order arrays.

Another look now at monadic ⍴, called the shape or size function, reveals that in general it yields a vector whose components give the number of components in each dimension of an array. So ⍴*PPR* is 15 7 or the structure of *PPR*. The number of components in *PPR* is ×/⍴*PPR* and the number of dimensions of *PPR* or the <u>rank</u> of *PPR* is ⍴⍴*PPR*. ⍴*M* is 3 4. The number of components in *M* is ×/⍴*M* or 12 and the rank of *M* is ⍴⍴*M* or 2.

The right argument of restructure can be a single number, a vector, or a matrix. If the right argument is a matrix, the components are taken from the matrix by rows. For example, try:

```
√   5⍴3                     5⍴2 7 5
√   2 4⍴3                   2 4⍴2 7 5
√   12⍴M                    3 3⍴M
```

When constructing a large matrix using restructure, it sometimes happens that the data of the right argument is too voluminous to fit on one line. If this should be the case, the right argument can be constructed as a vector using specification and catenation and then restructure can be used. For example:

```
√   B←23 5 7 8 9 123 5 7 8 3 5 9 56 89 2.3 7.89 24 7 9.08
√   B←B,5 7.89 6 9 2 1 7 9 4 6 8 9 1 2 6 7 8
√   B←6 6⍴B
√   B
```

A component of a matrix can be changed by specification. For example, to change the component in the second row, third column of *M* from 7 to 14, type:

```
√   M[2;3]←14
√   M
```

To change the components in the third row, first, third, and fourth columns from 2 8 3 to ¯5 7 ¯9, type:

```
√   M[3;1 3 4]←¯5 7 ¯9
√   M
```

In general, the replacement data must have the same shape as what it is replacing or must be a single component (which is used repeatedly). This means that if a matrix of data is to be replaced, it must be replaced by a matrix of data (or a single component). For instance, to change *M*[1 2;2 3] which is now

```
9 7
2 1
```

to

```
6 5
4 3
```

type:

```
✓   M[1 2;2 3]←2 2⍴6 5 4 3
✓   M
```

To change a row or a column, indicate that row or column in the index expression to the left of a specification. The expression:

```
✓   M[;3]←56
✓   M
```

makes every component of column 3 of *M* a 56. The expression:

```
✓   M[2;]←7 9 12 5
✓   M
```

replaces the components in row 2 with 7 9 12 5.

EXERCISES II

2. Write expressions for the following. Check yourself on the terminal.

   a. The matrix *SM* shown below.

```
 9   7   8   4
 6   2   1  13
 5  12  17   2
```

   b. The matrix *TR* shown below.

```
 3   6   9
12  15  18
21  24  27
```

c. The matrix *UW* shown below.

```
¯6  ¯12   9
 2    7  ¯1
 4    6   3
```

d. The matrix *L* shown below.

```
1  0  1  0
1  0  1  0
1  0  1  0
```

e. The vector *B* shown below.

```
1 3 ¯1 1 3 ¯1 1 3 ¯1
```

f. The vector *C* shown below.

```
4 9 8 7 4 9 8 7 4 9
```

g. The structures of each of the arrays created in (a) through (f) above.

h. Replace 17 in matrix *SM* with 49.

i. Replace column 2 of *TR* with 7 16 25.

j. Replace row 1 of matrix *L* with 14 12 6 9.

k. Replace the first two rows, last two columns of *SM* with 5 7 6 3.

l. Replace the main diagonal (upper left to lower right) of *TR* with 4 8 16. Hint: You may need repeated specifications.

3. The directions for finding postage using the parcel post table discussed in the first section were:

> To compute postage, add the ounces together and change the total to pounds, rounding up. After you have the total pounds, add one pound to your total for padding. Check the total with the chart for the postage to your local zone.

Define a function with header *A←ZONE POSTAGE OZ*, where *OZ* is a vector of ounces (weights of the various purchases) and *ZONE* is the delivery zone to compute postage. Use matrix *PPR* for the postal rates. Check your function by executing:

```
4 POSTAGE 5 7 9 11

6 POSTAGE 1 4 29

2 POSTAGE 105 34
```

Section 6.3 OPERATIONS ON MATRICES

We have already seen that indexing and shape operate on matrices as well as vectors. In fact, all of the primitive functions that operate on vectors extend to matrices. These extensions are of two kinds. The first set of functions, consisting of

```
+ - × ÷ ⌈ ⌊ | * = < ≤ ≥ > ≠ ∨ ∧ ~
```

operate on each of the components of a vector, that is, component-by-component. These functions are called scalar functions. (Since they are first defined for scalar arguments and then extend to vectors component-by-component; that is, treating each component in the vector like a scalar.) If the arguments are matrices, the function operates on the matrices component-by-component. For example,

```
if M is 3  4 and N is 2  9
        7  2          3  7

      M+N
5  13
10  9
```

That is,

```
      M[1;1]+N[1;1]             M[1;2]+N[1;2]

      M[2;1]+N[2;1]             M[2;2]+N[2;2]
```

The matrices must have the same structure, that is, for *A* fn *B*, where *A* and *B* are both matrices

```
      ∧/(ρA)=ρB
```

For example, try:

√	W←3 3ρ9?9
√	W
√	X←3 3ρ9?9
√	X

```
√     W×X
√     Y←2 3ρ6?6
√     Y
√     W+Y
```

The error report in response to the last expression indicates that the two matrices do not have the same shape.

It is also possible to have one argument a single number and the other a matrix, just as it was possible to have one argument a single number and the other a vector. For example, try:

```
√     3+W
√     ¯2×X
√     Y÷5
```

It is not possible to have one argument a vector and the other a matrix.

The monadic functions reciprocal, absolute value, roll, floor, ceiling, negation, factorial, and not also operate on matrices component-by-component. For example, try:

```
√     ÷3 3ρι9
```

EXERCISES III

4. Enter the following matrices so that you can check your work at the terminal.

```
M1←3 3ρ3 8 5 4 7 13 5 6 2

M2←3 4ρ¯9 6.1 3 ¯1.9 7 5.3 ¯2.1 4 6.1 3 4 8

M3←3 3ρ¯3 2 3.1 8.7 ¯4 6.4 ¯8 ¯1.7 3

M4←3 4ρ6 9 15 ¯3.1 ¯2 1 7.1 3 ¯8 5.9 ¯9 8

M5←2 3ρ1 2 3 4 5 6
```

Write expressions for the following using matrices *M*1, *M*2, *M*3, *M*4, and *M*5.

a. The sum of *M*1 and *M*3.

b. A 2 by 3 matrix of the factorials from 1 through 6.

c. A 2 by 3 matrix of the reciprocals of the numbers 1 through 6.

d. The absolute value of *M*3.

e. The difference between *M*2 rounded up and *M*4 rounded down.

f. *M*1 divided by 12.

g. *M*4 less than or equal *M*2.

5. (optional) Using matrices *M*1 and *M*3 <u>or</u> *M*2 and *M*4, try on the terminal

```
M1@M3          or          M2@M4
```

where the @ is replaced each time with one of the following scalar functions < ≤ = ≥ > ≠ - ÷ ⌈ ⌊ + × ⋆.

The second set of functions called <u>mixed functions</u>--/ +/ ⌽ and so forth--operate on vectors and matrices in a variety of ways. For instance, some of these operate along a coordinate of the matrix; that is, either on the rows, the first coordinate, or on the columns, the second coordinate. For the functions compression, reversal, rotation, reduction, and catenation the means of indicating which coordinate is affected is by qualifying the function symbol with the coordinate number. Let us look at reversal, for example. Specify the matrix *M* to be:

```
9   7   ¯6   ¯5
2   1   ¯7   ¯4
0.2 0.7 ¯0.8 ¯0.3
```

If we wish to reverse each column of *M* so that the resulting matrix looks like:

```
0.2 0.7 ¯0.8 ¯0.3
2   1   ¯7   ¯4
9   7   ¯6   ¯5
```

the row coordinate 1 should be indicated by qualifying the function:

```
⌽[1]M
```

If we wish to reverse each row of *M* so that the resulting matrix looks like:

```
¯5   ¯6   7   9
¯4   ¯7   1   2
¯0.3 ¯0.8 0.7 0.2
```

the column coordinate 2 should be indicated by qualifying the function:

```
⌽[2]M
```

Since operations are typically performed that affect the columns, the column qualifier may be omitted. If no qualifier is given, columns are assumed. Thus, ⌽*M* is equivalent to ⌽[2]*M*.

You might wonder why the column qualifier is indicated in order to reverse the rows. To answer this question, look at the indices of each component in the result in terms of the argument.

```
M[1;4]    M[1;3]    M[1;2]    M[1;1]

M[2;4]    M[2;3]    M[2;2]    M[2;1]

M[3;4]    M[3;3]    M[3;2]    M[3;1]
```

As you can see, reversing a row affects the column coordinate. And it is the column coordinate that is indicated in the function qualifier. Similarly reversing a column affects the row coordinate.

Reduction on matrices works like reversal on matrices. The function symbol is qualified and the reduction occurs along the specified coordinate. For example, try:

```
√   +/[1]M

√   +/M

√   ⌈/[1]M

√   ⌈/M
```

Compression and rotation are both dyadic mixed functions which are qualified. For each, only the right argument may be a matrix. The left argument is a single number or a vector. For both, if the left argument is a vector, the number of components in the left argument must be equal to the number of rows or columns in the right argument. That is, for *A*/[*Q*]*B* or *A*⌽[*Q*]*B*, (⍴*A*)↔(⍴*B*)[*Q*]. For compression, the rows or columns corresponding to ones in the left argument are selected. For example, try:

```
√   1 0 1/[1]M
√   1 0 1 0/M
```

For rotation, the components of the rows or columns are rotated according to the corresponding component of the left argument. For example, try:

```
√   1 2 3⌽[1]M
√   2 1 2 1⌽M
√   1 ¯2 ¯3⌽[1]M
```

If the left argument of rotation is a single number, each row or column is rotated that amount. For example, try:

```
√   2⌽[1]M
√   ¯1⌽M
```

For catenation, a matrix receives additional row(s) if the qualifier is 1 and additional column(s) if the qualifier is 2 (or omitted). When catenating two matrices, the number of rows must be the same if the qualifier is 2, and the number of columns must be the same if the qualifier is 1. For example, with:

```
√   M←2 3⍴6?6
√   M
√   N←3 3⍴9?9
√   N
√   L←2 4⍴8?8
√   L
```

Try:

√	M,[1]N	M,L
√	L,[1]¯3 ¯2 ¯7 ¯4	L,¯8 ¯9
√	¯3 ¯2 ¯7 ¯4,[1]L	¯8 ¯9,L
√	M,7	N,N
√	M,[1]7	N,[1]N

Membership, indexing, shape, and restructure of the mixed functions introduced that work on matrices are not qualifiable functions. Indexing, shape, and restructure are discussed in sections 6.1 and 6.2. For membership, the result is an array of the same shape as the left argument made up of ones and zeros depending on whether the corresponding element of the left argument is present in the right argument. For example, try:

√	N←3 2⍴9 8 ¯6 5 10 0
√	M∊N
√	N∊M

The functions index generator and dyadic random only operate on single numbers. They do not operate on vectors and do not operate on matrices.

EXERCISES IV

6. Using the matrices *M*1, *M*2, *M*3, and *M*4 of Exercise 4, write expressions for the following:

a. A matrix of ones and zeros showing which components of *M*1 are also components of *M*2.

b. The columns of *M*4 rotated one position to the left.

c. The rows of *M*3 reversed.

d. Eliminate the second row of *M*2.

e. Eliminate the first and fourth columns of *M*4.

f. Add down the columns of *M1*.

g. Add across the rows of *M1*.

h. The largest number in each row of *M4*.

i. The largest number in *M4*.

j. The smallest number in each column of *M2*.

k. The smallest number in *M2*.

Section 6.4 CHARACTER MATRICES

Matrices, like vectors, can have character components. A character matrix is created by using dyadic ρ, where the left argument is the shape of the array and the right argument is the vector of characters. Character matrices are displayed with no extra spaces between components. Try:

```
√    2 5ρ'GLASSTABLE'

√    5 5ρ'/---\|o o|| ^ ||\_/|\---'
```

EXERCISES V

7. Enter the following statements and you will see the development of a character matrix design:

```
√    DES←10 10ρ'-'

√    DES

√    DES[4 5 6 7;4 5 6 7]←'*'

√    DES

√    DES[3 8;3 4 5 6 7 8]←'⎕'

√    DES

√    DES[4 5 6 7;3 8]←'⎕'

√    DES
```

a. Create a character matrix in the shape of an American flag.

b. Create a stick man like the one shown below. Hint: You will need to use the blank character.

```
 o
\'/
 0
/ \
```

c. Create a frowning face.

8. Make a word list of the months of the years.

Section 6.5 SUMMARY

Matrices. A matrix is a two-dimensional array arranged like a table. The components of a matrix can be either numeric or character. Matrices are indexed by a two-part index

M[*R*;*C*]

The first index specifies the row; the second index specifies the column. The shape of a matrix can be found by ρ*M*. The first component of the vector result is the number of rows; the second component of the vector result is the number of columns.

A matrix is created by using the dyadic restructure function

(*R*,*C*)ρ*B*

The first component of the left argument is the number of rows in the result matrix; the second component is the number of columns in the result matrix. The data for the matrix is contained in the right argument. The right argument may be either numeric or character. The number of components in the left argument of restructure determines the rank or number of coordinates in the result array. One component is a vector; two components are a matrix; three components are a third-order array; and so forth.

Functions that have been shown as operating on vectors also operate on matrices. For the scalar dyadic functions

+ - ÷ × ⌈ ⌊ ⋆ < ≤ = ≥ > ≠ | ∧ ∨

The matrices must have the same shape, that is, the same number of rows and columns. The mixed dyadic functions compression, catenation, and rotation and the mixed monadic functions reduction and reversal must be qualified to indicate whether the operation is performed along rows or along columns. For example, ⌽[1]*M* indicates that reversal will occur along the first coordinate or rows. If the function is to be performed along columns, where the qualifier is [2], it may be omitted.

Section 6.6 SOLUTIONS TO THE EXERCISES

1. (a) PPR[7;6]
   (b) PPR[3 10;7]
   (c) PPR[4 6 12;3 4]
   (d) PPR[;5]
   (e) PPR[9;]
   (f) PPR[15;2]-PPR[1;1]
   (g) 5×PPR[11;6]
   (h) PPR[;5]-PPR[;7]

2. (a) SM←3 4ρ9 7 8 4 6 2 1 13 5 12 17 3
   (b) TR←3 3ρ3×⍳9
   (c) UW←3 3ρ¯6 ¯12 9 2 7 ¯1 4 6 3
   (d) L←3 4ρ1 0
   (e) B←9ρ1 3 1
   (f) C←10ρ4 9 8 7
   (g) ρSM | ρTR | ρUW | ρL | ρB | ρC
   (h) SM[3;3]←49
   (i) TR[;2]←7 16 25
   (j) L[1;]←14 12 6 9
   (k) SM[1 2;3 4]←2 2ρ5 7 6 3
   (l) TR[1;1]←4
       TR[2;2]←8
       TR[3;3]←16

3.
```
∇A←ZONE POSTAGE OZ;D
[1]    A←⍳0
[2]    →0×⍳15<D←1+⌈(+/OZ)÷16
[3]    A←PPR[D;ZONE]
  ∇
```

Note: Answers to the test problems are: .75, 1.10, 1.05. If your function gives these answers, it is probably correct even if not identical to the one shown above.

4. (a) M1+M3
   (b) !M5
   (c) |M3
   (d) ÷M5
   (e) (⌈M2)-⌊M4
   (f) M1÷12
   (g) M4≤M2

6. (a) M1∊M2
   (b) 1⌽M4

(c) `⌽[1]M3`

(d) `0 1 1 0/M4`

(e) `1 0 1/[1]M2`

(f) `+/[1]M1`

(g) `+/M1`

(h) `⌈/M4`

(i) `⌈/⌈/M4`

(j) `⌊/[1]M2`

(k) `⌊/⌊/M2`

7. (a) As an example:

```
FLAG←13 30ρ'~'
FLAG[⍳5;⍳10]←'*'
```

(b)

```
MAN←4 3ρ' '
MAN[1 2 3;2]←'o''0'
MAN[2 4;1 3]←'\//\'
```

(c) `5 5ρ'/---\|o o|| ∧ ||/¯\|\---'`

8.

```
M←'JANUARY  FEBRUARY MARCH    APRIL    MAY      JUNE     '
M←M,'JULY     AUGUST   SEPTEMBEROCTOBER  NOVEMBER DECEMBER '
MONTHS←12 9ρM
```

<u>Note</u>: A vector of the data was created first because the length of data exceeded the width of the paper. Once the vector of data was created, it was restructured into the appropriate matrix.

LESSON 7 USING MATRICES AND OTHER APL CAPABILITIES

In this concluding lesson, a problem using matrices is solved, additional APL primitive functions are introduced, and another form of input within a defined function is discussed.

Section 7.1 SOLVING A PROBLEM

```
 S
LESSON
 V
 E
 N
```

Let's define a function *CROSS* to build a crossword arrangement of two words like that above.

What we need:

1. A means of locating the common letters.
2. A means of properly arranging the two words.

Other Considerations:

1. What to do if there are no common letters in the two words.
2. What to do if there is more than one common letter in the two words.

The major functions needed to define *CROSS* are:

· Membership *A∊B* along with *+/B* to determine whether there are any letters in common between the two words

• <u>Compression</u> *A/B* and index generator ι*B* to determine the index numbers of the common letters in one word

• <u>Restructure</u> *A*ρ*B* to build the matrix (grid) to accommodate two words

• <u>Shape</u> ρ*B* to determine the length of each word

• <u>Indexing</u> *A*[*B*] to place the words in the proper place in the matrix

• <u>Roll</u> ?*B* to select one common letter randomly as the cross point. (This is not essential. We could also select the first or last or any common letter as the cross point.)

• <u>Index-of</u> *A*ι*B*, a new function, to determine the positions of the common letters in the second word.

Let us look at dyadic ι, the index-of function. Try the following expressions at the terminal and study the results:

√	7 4 6 8 2ι2	5 9 3 1ι5
√	9 8 6ι8	9 8 6ι7
√	9 8 6ι8 7	8 7ι9 8 6
√	7 9 5 3 7ι7	7 9 5 3 7ι7 7
√	*M*←2 2ρ9 6 4 3	*M*
√	6 2 9 4ι*M*	*M*ι6 2 9 4

You should have observed that dyadic ι looks for the right argument in the left argument and returns the index location of the right in the left. So, in the first example, 2 (the right argument) is the fifth number in the left argument and the result is 5. In the second, 5 is the first number in the left argument and the result is 1. In the fourth example, 7 is not found in the vector 9 8 6 and the result is 4, one more than the number of components in the left argument; that is, on no match the result is 1+ρ*V*, where *V* is the vector left argument. In the examples 7 9 5 3 7ι7 and 7 9 5 3 7ι7 7 where the right argument occurs more than once in the left argument, only the index number of the first occurrence is given. So, 7 9 5 3 7ι7 7 has a result of 1 1. As you saw in the last example, the left argument cannot be a matrix.

Returning once more to defining the function *CROSS*, we will use the header *∇GRID←X CROSS Y* where *GRID* is the matrix of crossed words *X* and *Y*; *X* is the horizontal word, and *Y* is the vertical word. The development of the defined function *CROSS* is given below.

Enter function definition mode:

```
      ∇GRID←X CROSS Y
```

Initialize the resultant:

```
[1]   GRID←''
```

If there are no matching letters, function execution will stop and the result will be the empty vector:

```
[2]   →3×∨/X∊Y
```

or

```
[2]   →0×⍳0=+/X∊Y
```

Either statement 2 will produce the same effect. In the first, the branch is to the next statement if there is at least one 1 in *X∊Y*. In the second, the branch is out of the function if all the components of *X∊Y* are zero.

Build the grid to accommodate the *X* and *Y* words. It must have ⍴*X* columns and ⍴*Y* rows:

```
[3]   GRID←((⍴Y),⍴X)⍴' '
```

Determine index numbers of the matching letters in *X*:

```
[4]   WX←(X∊Y)/⍳⍴X
```

Determine index numbers of those same letters in *Y*:

```
[5]   WY←Y⍳X[WX]
```

Select one common letter:

```
[6]   CL←?⍴WX
```

Place the *X* word in the grid:

```
[7]   GRID[WY[CL];]←X
```

Place the *Y* word in the grid:

```
[8]   GRID[;WX[CL]]←Y
```

End function definition:

```
[9]   ∇
```

The function *CROSS* as it is defined above is in the workspace *LESSONS*. Copy it into your workspace:

```
√     )COPY ___________* LESSONS CROSS
```

Then display the function:

```
√     ∇CROSS[⎕]∇
```

Try the function with:

```
√     'LESSON' CROSS 'SEVEN'
√     'POOR' CROSS 'JUD'
```

EXERCISES I

1. The function *CROSS* demonstrates the use of structuring and indexing of matrices in building the resultant. Another use of matrices, as suggested in Lesson 6, is the matrix as a table of information. The following exercise will give you practice in using matrices in both ways.

Define a function that prepares statistics on some students' performance on a test. The information collected is the number of problems worked, the number of correct problems, and the total time in minutes spent on the test. The test consists of *P* problems. Students are given a maximum of *T* minutes to work the problems, although they are told to work as fast as they can. Students are told that only problems worked will be considered for their scores. Let *P* and *T* be arguments of the function. Let each student be identified by a number--1, 2, 3,...,n.

The teacher is interested in getting the following information rounded to two decimal places:

General

1. The average number of problems worked
2. The average number of problems correct
3. The average time spent on the test

For Each Student

1. Score 1, percent problems correct÷problems worked
2. Score 2, percent problems correct÷*P*
3. Percent problems worked÷*P*
4. Average time per problem--problems worked÷*T*
5. Percent time spent÷time

The teacher would like the output table ranked so that the information for the student with the highest Score 1 is first, the next highest Score 1 second, and so on.

After you have defined your function, test your function out on the variable *DATA* with *P*←25 and *T*←20.

√)*COPY* ________* *LESSONS DATA*

DATA is a matrix with a row for each student. Column 1 is the student number, column 2 is the number of problems worked, column 3 is the number of correct, and column 4 is the time in minutes.

Make whatever corrections are necessary. When you are satisfied that your function works, compare your solution to the solution given at the end of the lesson. However, remember that it is not necessary that your solution duplicate the text solution. What is important is that your function gives the teacher all the information he wants.

Section 7.2 CHARACTER INPUT TO A FUNCTION

In Lesson 5 we defined a function *MULTIPLY* that drilled a student on his multiplication tables. Recall that a right-hand quad was used to signify that the function execution was to be interrupted to accept some numeric input from the terminal, that is, by *ANS*←⎕. The value of *ANS* becomes the value of whatever expression is typed in when ⎕: appears. One of the problems with using numeric input in the program is that there is no way of determining whether the student answered the question 8×4, for example, with the number 32 or with the expression 8×4 since the computer assigns the value of the expression typed in to the variable *ANS*. Using the quote-quad, ⍞ (⎕ backspace ') is one means of overcoming that problem. The ⍞ on the right of a specification signals that the input from the terminal should be considered character data. The characters '8×4' are not the same as the characters '32' and so a way is available to be sure that the student does not answer by keying in the problem. (Note: When using character input, spaces are characters; thus, '   32' is not the same as '32').

When ⍞ is used in a function, there is no visual signal at the terminal that input is expected. The keyboard simply unlocks. Everything entered is considered character data. If you do not want to continue, but want to return to execution mode, type ⍞ (*O* backspace *U* backspace *T*).

If *MULTIPLY* is modified so that the input comes in as character data, the test expression *ANS*=*N*[*I*]×*X* for determining whether the student typed the right answer cannot be used without converting *ANS* to numeric data or converting *N*[*I*]×*X* to character data. (Recall that *N*[*I*] is the *I*th randomly selected number and *X* is the multiplication table being tested.)

Converting Character Data to Numeric Data. The expression 1+'0123456789'⍳*ANS* converts *ANS* to a numeric vector whose numbers are the same as the characters of *ANS*. Try:

```
√    ANS←'32'

√    1+'0123456789'⍳ANS
```

The next step is to convert the vector to a single number. To do this we take account of the place value of numbers. In order to make the vector 3 2 the number 32, we must multiply 3×10 and 2×1 and add the products (3×10)+2×1. The decode function ⊥ does this. If *A* is the base desired, and *B* is the vector, the result of *A*⊥*B* is the base-10 equivalent of *B* in the base *A*. We are dealing with base-10 numbers, so 10⊥3 2 will give the result we want. Try:

```
√    10⊥3 2

√    10⊥4 7 9

√    2⊥1 1 0 0
```

In the third example, the binary number 1100 is converted to its base-10 equivalent 12.

Converting a Number to Character Data. For *N* less than 9, the expression '0123456789'[0 1 2 3 4 5 6 7 8 9⍳*N*] will convert *N* to character data. Try:

```
√    N←8

√    C8←'0123456789'[(0,⍳9)⍳N]
```

```
√    C8
√    C8=N
```

But if *N* is greater than 9, the expression as shown above will not work. Verify this by trying:

```
√    N←19
√    C19←'0123456789'[(0,⍳9)⍳N]
```

To make this expression work, *N* has to be replaced with a vector of digits. For instance, suppose *N* is 32, then we would want to use 3 2 as the digits vector, giving:

```
√    '0123456789'[(0,⍳9)⍳3 2]
```

The expression 10 10⊤32 converts 32 into the vector 3 2. ⊤ is the encode function. *A*⊤*B* converts the decimal number *B* into a vector of its base-*A* equivalent. The vector *A* must have at least as many components as the base-*A* number has places; otherwise, the result will be truncated. Try:

```
√    10 10 10⊤479
√    10 10⊤479
√    10 10 10 10⊤479
```

How can you determine how many places are necessary to convert the number *B*? Adding 1 to the *A* log of *B* and then rounding down will give the right number of places, provided that *B* is not 0. The logarithm function is ⍟ (○ backspace ⋆). *A*⍟*B* produces the logarithm in base-*A* of *B*. Try:

```
√    10⍟100            ⌊1+10⍟100
√    10⍟34             ⌊1+10⍟34
√    B←34              ⌊1+10⍟B
√    ⌊1+10⍟B+B=0       B←0
√    ⌊1+10⍟B           ⌊1+10⍟B+B=0
```

The expression, then, that will convert a number to a character vector is '0123456789'[(0,⍳9)⍳((⌊1+10⍟R+R=0)⍴10)⊤R]. Try:

```
✓    R←345
✓    CR←'0123456789'[(0,⍳9)⍳((⌊1+10⍟R+R=0)⍴10)⊤R
✓    CR
✓    R=CR
```

As you can see, converting character data to numeric data requires fewer functions than converting numeric data to character data.

Section 7.3 THREE MORE PRIMITIVE FUNCTIONS

In Lesson 2 we discussed how indexing and catenation could be used to insert a number in a vector. For example to insert 12 between 9 and ¯7 in the vector NM←8 4 9 ¯7 5, we could use the expression NM[⍳3], 12, NM[4 5].

Suppose we want to insert a zero between each pair of components of NM. Clearly using indexing and catenation is less efficient than simply reentering the vector as NM←8 0 4 0 9 0 ¯7 0 5.

A better way is to use the dyadic function expansion \. In the expression A\B, A is a vector of ones and zeros like the left argument of compression. In expansion, however, each zero represents the place of an insertion of a 0 in a numeric vector B and the place of an insertion of a blank in a character vector B. Try, for example:

```
✓    NM←8 4 9 ¯7 5
✓    (9⍴1 0)\NM
✓    CM←'HAPPY'
✓    (9⍴1 0)\CM
```

There must be as many ones in the left argument as there are components in the right argument, that is (+/A)=⍴B.

By using expansion along with indexing numbers (or characters) can be inserted in a vector. Try, for example:

```
√   NM←(9⍴1 0)\NM
√   NM
√   NM[2×⍳4]←4 ¯5 ¯16 ¯2
√   NM
√   CM←(9⍴1 0)\CM
√   CM
√   CM[2×⍳4]←'∘'
√   CM
```

Expansion also works on rows or columns of a matrix. Try, for example:

```
√   M←3 4⍴12?12
√   M
√   0 1 0 1 0 1 0\[1]M
√   1 0 0 1 0 0 1 0 0 1\M
```

A specialized compression takes place when the first *N* or last *N* components of a vector or first *N* or last *N* rows or columns of a matrix are dropped. Consider:

```
√   NM←8 4 9 ¯7 5
√   0 0 1 1 1/NM
√   1 1 0 0 0/NM
```

Instead of using compression and having to set up a vector of leading or trailing ones, the function <u>drop</u> ↓ can be used. In *A*↓*B*, if *A* is positive, *A* components will be dropped from the front of the vector *B*. If *A* is negative, |*A* components will be dropped from the end of vector *B*. Try, for example:

```
√   2↓NM
√   ¯3↓NM
```

Alternatively, the function take ↑ can be used. In *A*↑*B* if *A* is positive, the first *A* components of *B* are the resultant. If *A* is negative, the last |*A* components of *B* are the resultant. Try, for example:

```
√   2↑NM
√   ¯3↑NM
```

A specialized expansion takes place if |*A* is greater than ρ*B* when using take. In this case, (|*A*)-ρ*B* zeros (or blanks for a character vector) are catenated to the front of *B* if *A* is positive and to the back of *B* if *A* is negative. Try, for example:

```
√   8↑NM
√   ¯8↑NM
√   C←'HAPPY'
√   CE←8↑C
√   CE
√   ρCE
√   CF←¯8↑C
√   CF
√   ρCF
```

Take and drop can be used with matrices. With a matrix right argument, the left argument must have two components--the first dealing with the rows of the matrix, the second with the columns. For example, try:

```
√   M←3 4ρ9 8 7 6 5 2 1 7 4 1 2 9
```

√	1 2↓M	4 6↑M
√	¯1 ¯1↓M	¯4 ¯6↑M
√	1 ¯2↓M	¯4 6↑M
√	¯1 2↓M	4 ¯6↑M
√	2 3↑M	0 0↓M
√	¯2 ¯3↑M	3 4↑M
√	¯2 3↑M	0 0↑M
√	2 ¯3↑M	5 5↓M

EXERCISES II

2. Using the following variables:

```
R←9 8 ¯7 6 3 ¯9 2 5

C←'ABCDEFGHI'

MR←2 4ρR

MC←3 3ρC
```

Write expressions for the following:

a. Insert a zero between each component of *R*

b. Insert a blank between every component of *C*

c. Insert a 10 after every second component of *R*, that is,

```
9 8 10 ¯7 6 10 3 ¯9 10 2 5 10
```

d. Insert a ⎕ before every third component of *C*, that is,

```
⎕ABC⎕DEF⎕GHI
```

e. Insert a row of tens between the two rows of *R*, that is,

```
 9  8 ¯7  6
10 10 10 10
 3 ¯9  2  5
```

f. Insert two columns of tens between the second and third columns of *MR*, that is:

```
9   8  10  10  ¯7  6
3  ¯9  10  10  ¯2  5
```

g. Insert the matrix 3 3ρ'*JKLMNOPQR*' to interlace with the rows of *MC*, that is:

```
ABC
JKL
DEF
MNO
GHI
PQR
```

h. Drop the first five components of *R*

i. Add five blanks to the front of *C*

j. Add two rows of zeros to the bottom of *MR*

k. Add a blank 2 by 3 matrix to the top of *MC*

l. Drop the last column and last row of *MC*

Section 7.4 SUMMARY

New APL Primitive Functions. The primitive functions introduced in Lesson 7 are defined below.

- Index-of *A*ι*B*

The result is a vector of the indices of *A* at which the components of *B* can be found. If a component of *B* is not found in *A*, the result for that component is 1+ρ*A*. If a component of *B* occurs more than once in *A*, only the index of the first occurrence is given. *A* cannot be a matrix. There are no restrictions on the rank of *B*.

- Decode *A*⊥*B*

The result is the base-10 equivalent of a number in base-*A* whose places are represented by components of *B*.

- Encode *A*⊤*B*

The result is a vector which represents an encoding of the base-10 number *B* into a base-*A* equivalent. Each component of *A* represents a place in the result, and so for a valid representation *A* must have enough components to accommodate all of the places of the result.

- Logarithm *A*⍟*B*

The result is the logarithm of *B* in the base *A*.

- Expansion *A**B*

A is a vector of ones and zeros with as many ones as there are components in *B*, if *B* is a vector, or rows (or columns) in *B*, if *B* is a matrix. There is no limit to the number or placement of zeros in the left argument. Wherever a one occurs in the left argument, the result contains the next available component (or row or column) of *B*; wherever a zero occurs, the result contains a zero if *B* is numeric or a blank if *B* is character data.

- Drop *A*↓*B*

If *B* is a vector, the result is the same as *B* with the first *A* components excluded if *A* is positive and the last |*A* components excluded if *A* is negative. If *B* is a matrix, *A* must be a two-component vector. The first component indicates the number of rows to drop, the second component indicates the number of columns.

- Take *A*↑*B*

If *B* is a vector, the result is the first *A* components of *B* if *A* is positive or the last |*A* components of *B* if *A* is negative. If (|*A*)>⍴*B*, zeros or blanks are used to fill out the result. If *A* is positive, zeros (or blanks) precede *B*; if *A* is negative, zeros (or blanks) follow *B*. If *B* is a matrix, *A* must be a two-component vector. The first component indicates the number of rows to take, the second component indicates the number of columns.

Character Input. The expression *V*←⍞ causes the keyboard to release. Anything entered to replace ⍞ (called quote-quad) is treated as character data and is assigned as character data to the variable *V*. To get out of a quote-quad keyboard release situation, type *O*̶ (*O* backspace *U* backspace *T*).

Section 7.5 SOLUTIONS TO THE EXERCISES

1. If the result of your function on the matrix *DATA* from __________ * *LESSONS* with *P*←25 and *T*←20 was

```
      25 STAT 20
AVERAGE PROBLEMS WORKED:   18.86
AVERAGE PROBLEMS CORRECT:   13.86
AVERAGE TIME SPENT ON TEST:   16.86
     5        100          84         84      0.95         100
     1         96          96        100      0.8           90
     2         93.33       56         60      1.33         100
     3         61.54       32         52      1.54          75
     6         60          60        100      0.8           60
     4         45.45       40         88      0.91          65
     7         45.45       20         44      1.82         100
```

Your function probably works correctly.

The development of the solution is shown below. It assumes that each row of the matrix *DATA* contains student number, number of problems worked, number of problems correct, time in minutes. Enter function definition:

```
      ∇OUT←P STAT T
```

Give general information:

```
[1]   'AVERAGE PROBLEMS WORKED:  ';RND AVG DATA[;2]
```

Note:

```
          ∇Z←RND X
       [1]  Z←.01×⌊.5+100×X
          ∇

          ∇Z←AVG X
       [1]  Z←(+/X)÷ρX
          ∇
```

```
[2]   'AVERAGE PROBLEMS CORRECT:  ';RND AVG DATA[;3]

[3]   'AVERAGE TIME SPENT ON TEST:  ';RND AVG DATA[;4]
```

Prepare student information: Set up the structure of *OUT*, the information matrix.

```
[4]   OUT←((ρDATA)[1],5)ρ0
```

Fill up the matrix: Insert student numbers.

```
[5]   OUT[;1]←DATA[;1]
```

Score 1 information:

```
[6]   OUT[;2]←RND 100×÷/DATA[;3 2]
```

Score 2 information:

```
[7]   OUT[;3]←RND 100×DATA[;3]÷P
```

Percent problems worked:

```
[8]   OUT[;4]←RND 100×DATA[;2]÷P
```

Average time per problem:

```
[9]   OUT[;5]←RND T÷DATA[;2]
```

Percent time spent:

```
[10]  OUT[;6]←RND 100×DATA[;4]÷T
```

Determine the order (indices) of the rearranged matrix:

```
[11]  NEWINDEX←SPSRT OUT[;2]
```

Note: *SPSRT* is a sort routine to get the index values of the scores in order to rank the matrix.

```
      ∇Z←SPSRT X;IV
[1]    Z←''
[2]    IV←(X=⌈/X)/⍳⍴X
[3]    Z←Z,IV
[4]    X[IV]←¯1
[5]    →2×⍳~∧/X=¯1
      ∇
```

Rearrange *OUT* according to *NEWINDEX*:

```
[12]  OUT←OUT[NEWINDEX;]
```

Note: The primitive monadic function ⍒*B* (called down grade) will give the index numbers of the argument *B* in descending order. So

```
      ⍒8  9  5  3  8
2  1  5  3  4
```

The primitive function ⍋*B* (called up grade) gives the index numbers of *B* in ascending order. So

```
      ⍋8  9  5  3  8
4  3  1  5  2
```

Statements 11 and 12 can be combined and replaced by

```
[11]  OUT←OUT[⍒OUT[;2];]
```

The completed function is stored in __________* *LESSONS*. The matrix *DATA* which is part of the group can be used to test it with *P*←25 *T*←20. To try it:

```
√      )COPY ______________* LESSONS LESSON7
√      25 STAT 20
```

An auxiliary function for putting in data is often useful when much data needs to be entered. The function *ENTER*, for example, lets the teacher enter each student's data separately. After all the data is entered, the function creates the matrix.

```
√      )COPY ______________* LESSONS ENTER
```

Display *ENTER* and try it out by creating a data matrix to test *STAT* with.

Similarly a function for correcting any erroneous data can be defined. To see one:

```
√      )COPY ______________* LESSONS CORRECT
```

Display *CORRECT* and try it out.

2. a. `(15⍴1 0)\R`

   b. `(17⍴1 0)\C`

   c. `T←(12⍴1 1 0)\R`

      `T[3×⍳4]←10`

      `T`

   d. `T←(12⍴0 1 1 1)\C`

      `T`

      `T[1 5 9]←'⎕'`

      `T`

e.
```
T←1 0 1\[1]MR
T[2;]←10
T
```

f.
```
T←1 1 0 0 1 1\MR
T[;3 4]←10
T
```

g.
```
T←1 0 1 0 1 0\[1]MC
T[2 4 6;]←3 3ρ'JKLMNOPQR'
T
```

h.
```
5↓R
```

i.
```
14↑C
```

j.
```
4 4↑MR
```

k.
```
5 6↑MC
```

l.
```
¯1 ¯1↓MC
```

APPENDIX A
FUNCTIONS AND VARIABLES REFERRED TO IN THE LESSONS

Lesson 2

Functions to enter are *GUESS BESTBUY TABLE*

```
     ∇ GUESS;ANS;X;I;COUNT
[1]    'THINK OF A NUMBER BETWEEN 1 AND 100.'
[2]    'I WILL GUESS IT BY ASKING 7 QUESTIONS TO BE ANS
       WERED EITHER YES OR NO'
[3]    'WHEN YOU HAVE YOUR NUMBER, PRESS THE RETURN KEY
       .'
[4]    I←(1,ρ⍞)[1]
[5]    COUNT← 32 16 8 4 2 1
[6]    X←50
[7]  G1:'QUESTION ';I
[8]    'IS YOUR NUMBER LESS THAN ';1⌈X⌊100
[9]    ANS← 1 ¯1[1+'Y'=1ρ⍞]
[10]   X←X+ANS×COUNT[I]
[11]   →(7>I←I+1)/G1
[12]   'QUESTION 7'
[13]   'IS YOUR NUMBER EQUAL TO ';1⌈X⌊100
[14]   →('Y'=1ρ⍞)/G2
[15]   'YOUR NUMBER IS ';X-1
[16] G2:'AH HA'
     ∇

     ∇ BESTBUY X
[1]    →2+0=2|ρX
[2]    →0,ρ□←'YOU DID NOT ENTER A PRICE AND QUANTITY FO
       R EACH ITEM.  TRY AGAIN.'
[3]    X←((0.5×ρX),2)ρX
[4]    'THE MOST ECONOMICAL ITEM IS ITEM ';(÷/X)⍳⌊/÷/X
     ∇
```

```
     ∇ Z←X TABLE Y
[1]    Z←XρY
     ∇
```

Lesson 3

Functions to enter are *DIFFERENCE MEAN SUPER RANGE*
Variables to enter are the vectors *BOB CAROL TED ALICE*
These should be grouped into the group *BOWL* in this way:
)GROUP BOWL DIFFERENCE MEAN SUPER RANGE BOB CAROL TED ALICE

```
     ∇ Z←DIFFERENCE X
[1]    Z←X-+/X÷ρX
     ∇

     ∇ Z←MEAN X
[1]    Z←(+/X)÷ρX
     ∇

     ∇ Z←SUPER B
[1]    Z←0⌈0.75×200-MEAN B
     ∇

     ∇ Z←RANGE N
[1]    Z←(⌈/N),-⌈/-N
     ∇

       BOB
128  109  143  123  166  162  98  162  113
       146  162  96  108  115  143  130  114
       147  172  118  124  170  122  98  159
       145  154  108  106  134  128  105  120
       127  129  133  121  140  131  137

       CAROL
120  106  126  129  179  116  143  172  160
       124  98  115  110  164  109  118  159
       114  177  121  129  162  114  135  131
       120  107  147  153  145  131  137

       TED
148  137  142  129  140  102  125  109  143
       197  145  109  98  162  121  96  107
       126  134  117  150  135  177  201  123
       101  113  129  162  87  128  127  101
       145  106  120  164  159  146  110
```

```
      ALICE
167  101  137  162  123  134  142  121  146
       145  118  134  147  101  128  122  145
       159  153  127  129  108  145  113  102
       101  178  137  120  125  133  110  110
       123  123  97
```

Lesson 4

Functions in this lesson to enter are *ROOT AROOT BROOT NON FN* These functions should be grouped into the group *EX4* in this way:
)*GROUP EX4 ROOT AROOT BROOT NON FN*

```
     ∇ ROOT X
[1]    X*0.5
     ∇

     ∇ AROOT X
[1]    →0×⍳X<0
[2]    X*0.5
     ∇

     ∇ Z←BROOT X
[1]    →0×⍳X<0
[2]    Z←X*0.5
     ∇

     ∇ Z←NON M
[1]    Z←M
[2]    →3×M<0
[3]    Z←M×M
     ∇

     ∇ Z←FN X
[1]    →3×⍳0=2|ρX
[2]    Z←X[⌈0.5×ρX]
[3]    Z←0.5×X[0.5×ρX]+X[1+0.5×ρX]
     ∇
```

Lesson 5

Functions to enter are *MULTIPLY SORT*

```
     ∇ MULTIPLY X;SC;I;ANS;N
[1]    'FOR EACH PROBLEM MULTIPLY THE TWO NUMBERS SHOWN
        AND TYPE THE ANSWER'
[2]    N←12?12
[3]    SC←0
[4]    I←1
[5]  M1:N[I],X
[6]    ANS←⎕
[7]    SC←SC+ANS=N[I]×X
[8]    I←I+1
[9]    →M1×⍳I≤12
[10]   'YOUR SCORE IS'
[11]   ⌊100×SC÷12
     ∇

     ∇ NL←SORT OL
[1]   L1:NL←NL,⌊/OL
[2]    OL←(OL≠⌊/OL)/OL
[3]    →L1×⍳0≠⍴OL
     ∇
```

Lesson 6

Variable to enter is the matrix *PPR*

```
       PPR
  0.5       0.6       0.6       0.65      0.7       0.8       0.85
  0.5       0.6       0.6       0.65      0.7       0.85      0.85
  0.5       0.65      0.7       0.75      0.85      0.95      1
  0.55      0.7       0.75      0.85      0.95      1.1       1.2
  0.55      0.75      0.8       0.9       1         1.2       1.4
  0.55      0.8       0.9       1         1.1       1.4       1.5
  0.6       0.9       0.95      1.1       1.3       1.5       1.7
  0.6       0.95      1         1.1       1.4       1.6       1.9
  0.65      1         1         1.2       1.5       1.8       2
  0.65      1         1.1       1.3       1.6       1.9       2.2
  0.65      1.1       1.2       1.4       1.7       2         2.4
  0.7       1.1       1.2       1.5       1.8       2.1       2.5
  0.7       1.2       1.3       1.5       1.9       2.2       2.7
  0.75      1.2       1.4       1.6       2         2.4       2.8
  0.75      1.3       1.4       1.7       2.1       2.5       3

       ⍴PPR
15   7
```

Lesson 7

The functions to enter are *STAT ENTER CORRECT RND SPSRT AVG CROSS*
The variable to enter is the matrix *DATA*
These should be grouped into the group *LESSON7* in this way:
)GROUP LESSON7 DATA STAT RND SPSRT AVG

```
      ∇ OUT←P STAT T
[1]     'AVERAGE PROBLEMS WORKED:  ';RND AVG DATA[;2]
[2]     'AVERAGE PROBLEMS CORRECT:  ';RND AVG DATA[;3]
[3]     'AVERAGE TIME SPENT ON TEST:  ';RND AVG DATA[;4]
[4]     OUT←((ρDATA)[1],6)ρ0
[5]     OUT[;1]←DATA[;1]
[6]     OUT[;2]←RND 100×÷/DATA[; 3 2]
[7]     OUT[;3]←RND 100×DATA[;3]÷P
[8]     OUT[;4]←RND 100×DATA[;2]÷P
[9]     OUT[;5]←RND T÷DATA[;2]
[10]    OUT[;6]←RND 100×DATA[;4]÷T
[11]    OUT←OUT[⍒OUT[;2];]
      ∇
```

```
      ∇ Z←ENTER;I;SD;R
[1]     'HOW MANY STUDENTS?'
[2]     R←⎕
[3]     Z←(R,4)ρ0
[4]     I←1
[5]     'NO., PROB. WORKED, NO. CORRECT, TIME'
[6]   E1:'ENTER DATA FOR STUDENT'
[7]     SD←⎕
[8]     →11×ι4=ρSD
[9]     'FOUR ITEMS NOT ENTERED.  REPEAT.'
[10]    →5
[11]    Z[I;]←SD
[12]    I←I+1
[13]    →E1×ιR≥I
      ∇
```

```
      ∇ S←SPSRT X;IV
[1]     Z←''
[2]     IV←(X=⌈/X)/ιρX
[3]     Z←Z,IV
[4]     X[IV]←¯1
[5]     →2×ι~∧/X=¯1
      ∇
```

```
      ∇ Z←CORRECT X;CI;A;I;TEMP
 [1]     Z←X
 [2]    C1:'ENTER ROW AND COLUMN OF ITEM OR 9999 TO QUIT'
 [3]     I←⎕
 [4]     →(I=9999)/0
 [5]     →C2×ι∧/(I≤ρX),(I>0),I=⌊I
 [6]     →(C1+1),ρ⎕←'CHECK ROW AND COLUMN NUMBERS AND TRY
          AGAIN'
 [7]    C2:'ENTER CORRECTION'
 [8]     CI←⎕
 [9]     TEMP←Z[I[1];]
 [10]    TEMP[I[2]]←CI
 [11]    TEMP
 [12]    'OK?  1 FOR YES OR 0 FOR NO'
 [13]    →C1×ι0=A←⎕
 [14]    Z[I[1];[ 2]]←CI
 [15]    →C1
      ∇

      ∇ Z←RND X
 [1]     Z←0.01×⌊0.5+100×X
      ∇

      ∇ Z←AVG X
 [1]     Z←(+/X)÷ρX
      ∇

         DATA
    1    25   24   18
    2    15   14   20
    3    13    8   15
    4    22   10   13
    5    21   21   20
    6    25   15   12
    7    11    5   20

         ρDATA
 7  4

     ∇ GRID←X CROSS Y
[1]     GRID←''
[2]     →3×∨/X∊Y
[3]     GRID←((ρY),ρX)ρ' '
[4]     WX←(X∊Y)/ιρX
[5]     WY←YιX[WX]
[6]     CL←?ρWX
[7]     GRID[WY[CL];]←X
[8]     GRID[;WX[CL]]←Y
     ∇
```

APPENDIX **B**

THREE PROBLEMS REQUIRING LONGER SOLUTIONS

The problems and exercises in the lessons have been designed to give you practice with the particular functions under discussion. Solutions were provided so that you could see how the functions were used if you had any trouble with any of the problems.

Defined functions are, however, often self-correcting. When a function is entered into the system and is tested, you see without consulting an answer book whether it works or not. The first thing you find out is whether the expressions are acceptable in APL (because of the error detecting routines in APL). The next thing you find out is whether the result produced is the anticipated one. It is this that tells you that your solution is correct.

The following three problems are presented without solution. Each can be solved in several ways and each uses many of the APL functions discussed in these lessons. The statement of the problem is purposely general, so that you can have the fun of establishing the rules and details you want in the solution.

1. Develop a stock market game. Things you might consider: buying on margin--having some stocks more speculative than others--odd and round lot brokerage fees--market analysis prior to buying--number of stocks on the exchange.

2. Develop a game to play hangman (hang the butcher) or some other word guessing game.

3. Some people are always forgetting appointments, birthdays, anniversaries, etc. Establish a reminder program so that a "things to do" list for a given period gets printed.

APPENDIX C
APL PRIMITIVE FUNCTIONS DISCUSSED IN THE LESSONS

Function Symbol and Syntax	Function Name	Meaning	Discussed in Section
|*B*	Absolute Value	The magnitude of *B*	3.7
A+*B*	Addition	The sum of *A* and *B*	1.2 6.3
A∧*B*	And	Logic-and	5.3
→*B*	Branching	Go to statement whose value is *B*	4.1
A,*B*	Catenation	Append *B* to *A*	2.4 6.3
⌈*B*	Ceiling	*B* rounded up to an integer	4.1 4.6
A/*B*	Compression	Select components of *B* corresponding to ones in *A*	5.1
A?*B*	Deal	*A* random integers selected from one through *B*	5.2

Function Symbol and Syntax	Function Name	Meaning	Discussed in Section
A⊥B	Decode	Base-10 equivalent of B in base-A	7.2
A÷B	Division	Quotient of A and B	1.2 6.3
⍒B	Down Grade	The indices of B needed for sorting B in descending order	7.6
A↓B	Drop	The first (if A>0) or last (if A<0) |A components of B are eliminated	7.2
A⊤B	Encode	A representation of base-10 number B in base-A	7.2
A=B	Equal	1 if true; 0 if false	4.1
A\B	Expansion	Inserting zeros (or blanks) in B corresponding to zeros in A	7.2
!B	Factorial	B factorial	3.4 6.3
	Floor	B rounded down to the nearest integer	4.1
A>B	Greater than	1 if true; 0 if false	4.1
A≥B	Greater than or equal	1 if true; 0 if false	4.1
⍳B	Index Generator	Integers from one through B	2.5

Function Symbol and Syntax	Function Name	Meaning	Discussed in Section
A[*B*]	Indexing	The *B* components of *A*	2.4 6.1
A⍳*B*	Index-of	Index positions of *B* in *A*	7.1
A<*B*	Less than	1 if true; 0 if false	4.1
A≤*B*	Less than or equal	1 if true; 0 if false	4.1
A⍟*B*	Logarithm	$\text{Log}_A B$	7.2
A⌈*B*	Maximum	The greater of *A* and *B*	3.4 6.3
A⌊*B*	Minimum	The lesser of *A* and *B*	3.4 6.3
A∊*B*	Membership	1 if *A* is present in *B*; 0 otherwise	5.3
A×*B*	Multiplication	Product of *A* and *B*	1.2 6.3
-*B*	Negation	The negative of *B*	3.4 6.3
A≠*B*	Not equal	1 if true; 0 if false	4.1
A⋆*B*	Power	*A* raised to the *B* power	3.4 6.3
~*B*	Not	1 if *B* is 0; 0 if *B* is 1	5.3
A∨*B*	Or	Logic-or	5.3

Function Symbol and Syntax	Function Name	Meaning	Discussed in Section
÷*B*	Reciprocal	1÷*B*	3.4 6.3
fn/*B*	Reduction	Insert fn between elements of *B* and evaluate expression	3.2 3.4 6.3
A∣*B*	Remainder	Remainder of *B*÷*A*	4.1 4.6
A⍴*B*	Restructure	The data of *B* arranged in an array of shape *A*	6.2
⌽*B*	Reversal	*B* in reverse order	5.3 6.3
?*B*	Roll	A random number from 1 through *B*	5.2
A⌽*B*	Rotation	The elements of *B* rotated ∣*A* positions to the left (if *A*>0) or right (if *A*<0)	5.3 6.3
⍴*B*	Shape	The number of elements in each dimension of *B*	3.2 6.2
A←*B*	Specification	Variable *A* is assigned value of *B*	2.2 6.2
A-*B*	Subtraction	Remainder of *A* less *B*	1.2 6.3
A↑*B*	Take	The first (if *A*>0) or last (if *A*<0) ∣*A* components of *B*	7.2
⍋*B*	Up Grade	The indices of *B* needed to sort *B* in ascending order	7.6

BIBLIOGRAPHY

"APL: The Controversial, Powerful Interactive Language", Computing Newsletter for Instructors of Data Processing, Vol. IV., No. 7 (March, 1971). Colorado Springs, 80909: Box 9630, pp 1-2.

"APL--The Language of the 4th Generation?", Computing Newsletter for Instructors of Data Processing, Vol. V. No. 7 (March, 1972), Colorado Springs, 80909: Box 9630, pp 1-2.

APL ⍞ -- The APL Quote-Quad is an informal publication of APL users. It contains short articles, programming notes, signed opinion, announcements, conference summaries, and so forth. Subscription information can be obtained from Garth H. Foster/Syracuse University/Syracuse, New York, USA.

Berry, P.C., Falkoff, A.D., & Iverson, K.E., Using the Computer to Compute: A Direct But Neglected Approach to Teaching Mathematics, New York, New York: IBM New York Scientific Center Report #320-2988, May, 1970.

McCracken, David, "Whither APL?" in Datamation (September 15, 1970) pp 53-57.

Pakin, Sandra, APL/360 Reference Manual (2nd. edition), Chicago, Illinois: Science Research Associates, 1972.

Redwood, Peter H.S., "APL for Business Applications" in Datamation (May, 1972) pp 82-86.